Girls and Young Women

Entrepreneurs

True Stories About Starting
and Running a Business
Plus How You Can Do It Yourself

Frances A. Karnes, Ph.D.
and Suzanne M. Bean, Ph.D.

Edited by Elizabeth Verdick

free spirit
PUBLiSHiNG

Works
for kids

Library of Congress Cataloging-in-Publication Data

Karnes, Frances A.
   Girls and young women entrepreneurs : true stories about starting and running a business, plus how you can do it yourself / Frances A. Karnes and Suzanne M. Bean ; edited by Elizabeth Verdick.
      p.   cm.
   Includes bibliographical references and index.
   Summary: Profiles girls who have successfully started and run businesses, such as making and selling cheesecakes, inventing and marketing a kiddie stool, making and selling watercolor paintings. Includes a section on how to be an entrepreneur, and historical information about women in business.
   ISBN 1-57542-022-8
   1. New business enterprises—Juvenile literature.   2. Women-owned business enterprises—Juvenile literature.   3. Entrepreneurship—Juvenile literature. [1. Entrepreneurship.   2. Women in business.   3. Business enterprises.]   I. Bean, Suzanne M., 1957–   . II. Verdick, Elizabeth.   III. Title.
   HD62.5.K364   1997
   658.4'21'082—dc21   97–13535
                                                                              CIP
                                                                               AC

An earlier version of the story about Jeanie and Elizabeth Low, which appears on pp. 38–44, can be found in *Girls and Young Women Inventing: Twenty True Stories About Inventors Plus How You Can Be One Yourself* by Frances A. Karnes and Suzanne M. Bean (Minneapolis: Free Spirit Publishing, Inc., 1995).

The authors would like to thank Jenna Wedge, Avon Photography, for use of the photo that appears on p. 11; Dawn Matthews, First Light Communications, for the photo that appears on p. 76; and Anne White for the photo that appears on p. 95.

Cover design by Circus Design
Book design by Julie Odland Smith
Index prepared by Eileen Quam and Theresa Wolner

10 9 8 7 6 5 4 3 2 1

Printed in the United States of America

Free Spirit Publishing Inc.
400 First Avenue North, Suite 616
Minneapolis, MN 55401
(612) 338-2068
help4kids@freespirit.com

This book is dedicated to Mary Ryan Karnes and to Cameron Meriweather Bean, who wish to encourage girls and young women to become involved in entrepreneurship. This book is also dedicated to all young female entrepreneurs and to the adults who have encouraged them.

Acknowledgments

OUR DEEPEST APPRECIATION IS GIVEN TO THE YOUNG WOMEN IN THIS book, who have decided to share their stories with others who are interested in entrepreneurship and in business. We are also very grateful to the many organizations, associations, and individuals who responded to our search for young female business leaders. Interactions with and words of encouragement from these adults made us realize how important it is to continue our work in spotlighting the positive accomplishments of girls and young women. Some of the adults who assisted with our other two books about the accomplishments of girls called to thank us for our ongoing support and encouragement of young women. Thank you all for your assistance and kind words.

Judy Galbraith, our publisher, and her outstanding staff have always been available for technical assistance and support. We are indeed indebted to them for making this publication a reality.

Cathy Pentecost rendered invaluable assistance on several aspects of the book, Patti Rash helped with the various stages of manuscript preparation, Kristen Stephens assisted with technical knowledge, Jackie Williams typed the manuscript, and Barbara Van Duser oversaw the many aspects of the Center for Gifted Studies. We are grateful for their outstanding work.

We continue to have the support of the administration at the University of Southern Mississippi and the Mississippi University for Women. We are in nurturing university environments and are thankful to the administrators, our colleagues, the staff, and our students for their encouragement and help.

We are also very fortunate to have families who understand the importance of our work and, more specifically, our need to continue to write for girls and young women. To Ray Karnes and Mark Bean, our husbands, we offer our deepest appreciation for their love and patience. We are constantly reminded of the potential of future generations through Christopher, John, Leighanne, and Mary Ryan Karnes, and Meriweather and Hudson Bean.

Contents

Part Two: How to Be an Entrepreneur . . 127

Part Three: For Further Inspiration 147

Introduction

Entrepreneurs in Action

WHEN YOU HEAR THE WORD "ENTREPRENEUR," WHAT IMAGES COME to mind? Do you think of someone older—an adult? Someone who has years of business experience? Perhaps a man?

When you think of your future career, do you see yourself working for someone else?

If you answered yes to these questions, this book can help you to look at things differently. Instead of taking a traditional route as you embark on your career, you can consider becoming an entrepreneur. Owning your own business is a great way to achieve independence, earn money, and make a difference in the world. You don't have to wait until you're an adult to become an entrepreneur. Girls and young women across the country are starting businesses every day.

Girls and young women who explore entrepreneurship are following in the footsteps of the millions of women who, throughout history, have used their entrepreneurial skills to sell their unique products and services, and to earn money for themselves and their families. As early as 4000 B.C., women were traders, and they eventually became merchants, landowners, and business leaders. Although society didn't always welcome women in business, they persisted and established their own shops, inns, boardinghouses, companies, museums, magazines, newspapers, and factories.

Many of these female entrepreneurs not only created products made especially for women but also offered employment opportunities for other women. For example, Madame C. J. Walker,* an African

---

*To learn more about Madame C. J. Walker and other important women business owners, check out the list of recommended books on pp. 157–159, and the timeline that begins on p. 160.

1

American, headed for Denver in 1906 with less than two dollars in her pocket to start a company that produced hair products and cosmetics for black women. As her business grew, she hired thousands of sales agents, most of whom were African-American women. She eventually became a self-made millionaire. Like C. J. Walker, women in all parts of the world have discovered the value of entrepreneurship. Look around you. Women in your community and beyond have founded dynamic, successful businesses—Esprit, Jazzercise, Mary Kay, Gymboree, Weight Watchers, Discovery Toys, and the Body Shop, to name just a few. These names, products, or services may be a part of your everyday life.

What do all of these women have in common besides entrepreneurship? A vision, a dream, motivation, imagination, courage, and, most of all, the belief that nothing can stop them. We hope that this book will help inspire you to develop these traits in yourself and to follow *your* dream of entrepreneurship.

What Is an Entrepreneur?

An entrepreneur can be a woman, a man, a girl, or a boy. An entrepreneur can be age nine or age ninety. An entrepreneur can be the sole employee of a business or can have a staff of 500 or more. An entrepreneur can have one business or many. There are no limitations. If you want to start a business, don't think you have to wait until you're older and more experienced. Don't think you need to have thousands of dollars, a great office space, and lots of employees. If you want to start a business, do it. This book will tell you how.

One of the first steps is understanding what an entrepreneur is. An entrepreneur is the person responsible for starting a business, an organization, or an enterprise. An entrepreneur manages the business and assumes all of the risks involved. To get the business off the ground, the entrepreneur usually needs the following: an idea for a product or service, a business plan, start-up money, a location for the business, and knowledge of business and marketing basics. Other important aspects of running a business may include hiring staff, selecting and developing an inventory, keeping financial accounts accurate and current, and helping the business to grow.

Being an entrepreneur involves two key ingredients: *risk-taking* and *responsibility.* When you start and run a business, you take risks when determining whether your business idea will work, borrowing money for the business or investing your own money in it, and expanding the business. You take responsibility for the quality of your product or service, the satisfaction of your customers, all of the finances and the staff involved, and any mistakes that are made. Why would someone want to take such risks and take on so much responsibility? Because entrepreneurship also involves great *rewards.* Although starting a business requires courage and commitment (not to mention hard work!), you'll learn to:

- believe in yourself,
- act independently,
- be a decision-maker, and
- set goals and reach them.

You'll also:

- build your confidence,
- learn new skills,
- earn the respect and trust of your customers and peers, and
- achieve the satisfaction of doing something you believe in.

When your business succeeds, you'll know that it was because of *you.*

How to Use This Book

While reading this book, consider keeping a Business Notebook to record your thoughts and ideas. It can be a spiral notebook, loose pages in a binder, a blank book, or anything else you feel comfortable writing in. You could also use a computer, if you have access to one at home or at school.

This book contains three parts: "Female Entrepreneurs and Their Businesses," "How to Be an Entrepreneur," and "For Further Inspiration." As you read each section, take notes about the things that inspire you, advice you find valuable, business ideas that come to mind, mistakes you'd like to avoid, information that might help you with your business, and goals you'd like to set and achieve. Refer to your notebook whenever you're in search of ideas or inspiration.

Part One includes true stories of girls and young women who are entrepreneurs. The girls range in age from nine to twenty-five, and they come from different areas of the U.S., including Puerto Rico. One young woman is from Australia. Some of the girls own small businesses, while others run national organizations. A few of the young women have business partners. Some of the businesses are nonprofit (not for the purpose of making a profit), while some are earning more money than their owner ever dreamed possible. Their stories fall under "Product Businesses," if the main purpose is to sell a product, or "Service Businesses," if the focus is on providing a service to others.

All of the girls share their dreams, advice, mistakes, and successes. You'll read about their families and activities, the steps they took to establish their businesses, and their plans for the future. You'll learn about what motivates them and who has helped them along the way.

At the end of each group of stories, you'll find some questions to think about and ideas to try. Write your answers to the questions in your Business Notebook. Share the questions with other entrepreneurs, your family members, and your friends. See what they think, and use their ideas as a springboard for more of your own. Try the activities, too. They're designed to help you find ways to start a business and to make your business a success.

Part Two describes the many steps entrepreneurs take to start a business. You'll learn about developing the traits of a successful entrepreneur, protecting your ideas, naming your business, writing a business plan, and making sense of the legal issues that might affect you and your business. Reading and understanding this section of the book will help you to avoid some of the common pitfalls of entrepreneurship. The end of Part Two contains ten of our best tips for young entrepreneurs.

As you read this section, keep your Business Notebook handy. You can record a list of your entrepreneurial traits and the qualities you'd like to develop in yourself. You can brainstorm ideas for products and/or services. Use your notebook to develop a vision for your business and to keep track of your goals. Create an outline for your business plan, and collect the names of people who can help you to write, edit, and present the plan. For fun, keep a list of possible names for your business and designs for your logo. Refer to the list once you're ready to put your plans for a business into action.

In **Part Three**, you'll find facts and information about women entrepreneurs of yesterday and today. A timeline of women business owners in history shows their achievements and highlights the strides that women have made over the centuries. Quotes by contemporary women entrepreneurs shed light on the struggles they've endured, the lessons they've learned, and the secrets of their success.

We've provided many resources that offer information and support to potential entrepreneurs. There are biographies of entrepreneurs and books about starting and running a business. We've also listed some magazines and newsletters that address business issues, entrepreneurship, and money management. You'll find a list of organizations and associations that you can get in touch with by mail, phone, or FAX. Some of these organizations have their own Web sites that you can browse for more information.

Your Business Notebook is a great place to record the addresses and phone/FAX numbers of organizations that might be able to help you. Investigate their Web sites and print out any information that might be useful to store in your notebook. You can also use your notebook to start your own timeline of women in business. Find other female entrepreneurs who have inspired you, and do some research on the founding dates of their businesses. Or make a timeline about *you*. Record the founding date of your business and each success or learning experience. Lastly, use your notebook to collect quotes that you find helpful or meaningful. Try to think of your own quotes about entrepreneurship and make these your words to live by.

At the end of the book, you'll find a glossary that will help you to understand some basic business terms. Refer to the glossary whenever you come across a business vocabulary word that's unfamiliar to you.

Girls and young women who have established their own businesses have been and will continue to be outstanding role models for young females around the world. We congratulate each of them. We also congratulate *you* for considering entrepreneurship as a possibility for your future. Good luck!

Part One

Female Entrepreneurs and Their Businesses

Product Businesses

Lindsay and Stacey Elder

Thing-a-ma-dangles

Fourteen-year-old Lindsay Elder and eighteen-year-old Stacey Elder are sisters from Simsbury, Connecticut. Lindsay and Stacey are an energetic pair who pursue their goals with persistence and a strong determination to succeed. They're grateful to their parents—Stephen, who works for a computer consulting company, and Brenda, an office manager—for giving them full support in everything they try.

Lindsay is an eighth grader at Henry James Middle School, where she's captain of the dance team. Her favorite subject is math. Stacey currently attends Presbyterian College in Clinton, South Carolina, where she's a freshman. She works in the admissions office and belongs to Sigma Sigma Sigma sorority. Although Stacey originally started Thing-a-ma-dangles, Lindsay took over the business after her sister went away to college.

THING-A-MA-DANGLES BEGAN AS A GIRL SCOUT PROJECT FOR MY sister, Stacey, in sixth grade when she made a pair of earrings for our mom out of a material called Friendly Plastic. When Mom wore them to the office, her coworkers loved them and asked her for a pair. Stacey and I purchased some Friendly Plastic and began making jewelry. Our earrings, pins, bracelets, and barrettes were popular at Mom's office.

The following fall, we entered a large craft fair called September Fest, which was held in the center of Simsbury. At the time, I was seven and Stacey was twelve. Our booth was a card table covered with almost 200 pieces of jewelry. We never could have imagined the response we'd receive from our customers. People were constantly crowding around our display, amazed that two young girls could accomplish such a large project.

The craft fair opened many doors for us. We participated in more fairs, and by the time we were eight and thirteen, we had our jewelry, which we called Thing-a-ma-dangles, featured in several local stores. Our work became known around town, and we realized that we now had regular customers looking for our items. We expanded our horizons and created a line of women's blazers fashioned from men's sport coats and embellished with lace and fabric. This new creation was a hit at our third September Fest. Our display was transformed from a small card table to a full 8' × 10' tent-covered exhibit.

Soon we began working with a new medium, Fimo Clay, and we made earrings, necklaces, and bracelets. We were still selling our Friendly Plastic jewelry and our blazers, but these items had begun to go out of style. Although the Fimo Clay jewelry wasn't as

Stacey *(left)* and Lindsay Elder

Thing-a-ma-dangles jewelry

successful as the Friendly Plastic jewelry, it was still popular. We also started using pieces of antique jewelry to create pins, which our customers liked.

Our next new product was wooden massagers, and they were a success. We called them Thing-a-Massagers. They looked like wooden aliens, so we really had to go out and market them to get people interested. We gave people demonstration back rubs until our arms were sore! We had a lot of fun watching the expressions on our customers' faces as they received a free massage.

Because Stacey was so active in Junior Achievement and Thing-a-ma-dangles, she was featured in an article entitled "Tomorrow's Entrepreneurs" in *Newsweek* magazine. This honor opened many doors for her. She was accepted to prestigious colleges and was asked to speak at the Junior Achievement Businessmen's Hall of Fame. When Stacey went to college, she handed over Thing-a-ma-dangles to me. I now have full ownership of the business.

Running Thing-a-ma-dangles has always been a challenge. Stacey and I learned about the changing economy and how to budget our money. We had a checking account at an early age. Because our business required us to pay state sales tax,* we kept detailed records of all of our sales and expenses. The business has also brought many rewards. We learned to be organized and to achieve our goals. Thing-a-ma-dangles customers range from young to elderly women, and the products have quite a following in the local towns. Our customer loyalty has always made us feel very proud.

Many people have helped us over the years. Our parents have been wonderful, and I feel that we owe a lot of our success to them. Our mom has always been quick to offer new ideas for jewelry, and she's our best advertisement. Our dad has helped us to set up and take down the displays. Mom and Dad have both spent many hours sitting at craft fairs and carting the Thing-a-ma-dangles displays from town to town.

Over the years, Stacey and I learned that you can't *always* be successful. We showed our products at fairs where we barely broke even. We sat for many hours in the rain, trying to look cheerful. We watched people walk right by us without even giving us a glance. There were rude customers and screaming babies. We learned to be as nice as we could to even the most impolite people.

If you're thinking about becoming an entrepreneur, our advice is to stay committed to your project. Once you start, you have to see it through. You can't skip out because you're tired or show your customers that you're in a bad mood. You can't act shy or quiet—an entrepreneur needs to get out and sell her product with enthusiasm. And you can't just sit back and expect people to approach you. You have to display an air of confidence in yourself and in your product.

Having full ownership of Thing-a-ma-dangles is exciting and overwhelming. I find it hard to come up with new ideas all the time. There's a lot to keeping a business going, especially when you're only fourteen. I'd like to continue Thing-a-ma-dangles because it has opened so many doors for me. I hope it will open even more.

---

*To learn more about sales tax, see p. 145.

Jamie Hudson

Watercolors by Jamie

Jamie Hudson, a fourteen-year-old eighth grader, is a very talented and creative artist. She has a younger sister, Kathryn Ann, and a younger brother, Franklin. She lives with her family in the rural farming community of Holly Bluff, Mississippi. Her mother, Angela, is an elementary school teacher, and her father, Jimmy, works for the Mississippi Chemical Corporation.

Jamie is an honor student at Manchester Academy in Yazoo County. Her favorite subjects in school are art and English, and she's a member of the dance team. Jamie enjoys many hobbies, including singing, reading, dancing, and painting. She's also an active member of her church, where she sings in the choir.

M Y PAINTING BUSINESS ACTUALLY BEGAN BY ACCIDENT. I NEVER expected to use a talent and hobby that I love in order to make money. I paint and sell my own watercolors. I named my business Watercolors by Jamie.

I started painting when I was about two years old. My grandmother, Meme, put me in a high chair with paper and paints. She taught me how to look closely at things and to really see them. She also taught me how to mix and blend colors to get the results I wanted. My grandmother thought all of my artwork was wonderful. I still love to paint with Meme.

When I was four, I won my first art contest for a watercolor painting I called *Rainbows and Waterfalls*. Each year, I won or placed in the art contest at my school. Yazoo County Junior Auxiliary has been sponsoring an annual art contest for local

Jamie Hudson

artists since 1992. I entered a picture each year, and I won first place for my age group in 1992, 1993, and 1994.

In the 1996 contest, I won four ribbons with four different entries. Each of my paintings had some historical significance to Yazoo County. After this contest, several people wanted to purchase my paintings. I sold one to the Mississippi Chemical Corporation for display in their main office building. I sold the remaining three paintings to other local companies that wanted to display them.

Many people who saw my art asked if I could paint pictures for them. They wanted paintings of buildings, stores, houses, dogs, and many other things. My mom suggested that I start a business, and she had business cards and receipt forms printed for me. We set up a place in our house where I could paint and keep my supplies organized.

Jamie posing with some of her favorite paintings

The people around Yazoo County seemed to be mostly interested in paintings of old buildings, stores, churches, and houses. This gave me the idea to paint a collage containing different stores, buildings, and churches around Holly Bluff. It took me two weeks to complete the painting. While I was away at summer camp, my mom had the collage framed. She took it to a local bank in Holly Bluff for display, and the employees wanted the bank to buy the painting. We sold the painting for nearly two hundred dollars, and it now hangs in the bank.

That same day, people began calling to ask me to paint a picture of Holly Bluff for them, so I decided to paint another Holly Bluff scene. My mom made calls all over Mississippi, trying to find someone who could make a few inexpensive prints of my painting. To get the prints made, I had to estimate how many orders for the painting I actually had. I didn't want to buy a lot more prints than I could sell.

I got the prints made in August of 1996, and I sold sixty prints in three months. I spent about seven dollars to have each print made, and I'm selling them for twenty dollars each. This price includes the cost of my labor and supplies. So far, I've made about seven hundred dollars on the Holly Bluff painting.

About two weeks after painting and printing the Holly Bluff scene, I decided to paint a picture of a historic home called Mount Helena, which was built before the Civil War and was being restored in nearby Rolling Fork. We traveled the sixteen miles to Rolling Fork so I could begin painting. After I finished the piece, I had it framed. A friend of my mom's then took the painting to Rolling Fork to show it to the owners of Mount Helena. They loved the painting and immediately bought it.

Soon people from Rolling Fork began calling me to ask for their own Mount Helena painting. Because I had so many orders, I decided to paint another picture of Mount Helena and to make more prints. I had twenty prints made, and I've sold fifteen of them.

I recently painted *Mississippi Magnolia* for a competition open to children under eighteen years of age. The winner of the competition would get his or her artwork printed on the 1997 cover of the Delta Telephone Company phone directory. I was fortunate to win the contest, and I was paid one hundred dollars. The telephone

Jamie hard at work

directories will be in the hands of about a thousand people, which means I'll probably get lots of publicity for my business.

Next, I decided to approach several local gift shops to see if the owners would be interested in selling some of my work on consignment (meaning the gift shop owners would display my paintings to sell them; any unsold paintings would be returned to me). I talked to the owners of Gilbert's gift shop in Yazoo County and the Green Apple gift shop in Rolling Fork, and both stores agreed to the idea. The owners planned to charge a mark-up price of 33 percent to their customers.

I provided the stores with framed and matted pictures for display and with individual prints to sell. Because sales were good during the Christmas season, I've spoken with the owner of the Green Apple about doing an exclusive watercolor painting to be available only at that location.

My business has turned into more than just painting pictures. I've been hired to decorate cakes and birthday parties. People like to hire me to babysit, too, because I draw and paint with their children.

There are many advantages to having a business. I like earning money for myself, and I have my own checking and savings accounts at the bank. I put 10 percent of my earnings in the checking account, and the rest goes into savings. I use some of my earnings to pay business expenses such as printing, framing, and supplies. My parents help to monitor my spending. Sometimes it's hard to get a check cashed when you're not old enough to have a driver's license.

For three years, I've taken business leadership classes at the University of Southern Mississippi to learn more about entrepreneurship and running a business. The marketing strategies taught in these classes have made it possible for me to succeed. My parents continue to help me manage my business affairs. When I have a new idea, they always encourage me.

My advice to other young women who want to own a business is to find something you like to do and are good at, and use this as your starting point. Set goals for yourself, and follow through with your ideas. Be patient and keep trying. You *will* be successful.

Poppy King

Poppy Industries

Poppy King, age twenty-four, lives and works in Australia. At age eighteen, she started her own cosmetics business, which grew quickly and now employs nearly twenty-five people full-time. Poppy has been a member of the Small Business Council of Australia and is a well-known public speaker. She regularly makes presentations about her own business achievements and about issues of national interest to Australians. In 1995, Poppy was honored as Young Australian of the Year by the National Australia Day Council.

As a child, I often felt different from other people, as if I didn't fit in. My father died when I was seven, and my mother supported my brother and me by being a knitwear designer. We lived above a shop in the center of Melbourne in Australia. My mother has always made me feel proud to stand up for what I believe. She helped me to realize that sometimes when you stand out from the crowd you draw criticism, but this doesn't mean you've done anything wrong.

Many experiences throughout school were fundamental in shaping me as a person and giving me the courage to go against the norm and start my own business at a young age. I finished my high school education at a wonderful school that encouraged individuality. I put in average effort and got average results. I was always much better at learning from practice rather than theory.

By the time I finished school, I was unsure about what career I wanted to pursue. I wasn't too concerned about this indecision, though, because I knew I would eventually figure out what I wanted

Poppy King

to do. Because of my experiences working part-time in clothing boutiques and coffee shops, I knew I was capable of supporting myself.

During my first year out of school, I decided to enroll in some courses at a university. I took subjects like philosophy, psychology, media studies, and sociology. Because I had no clear direction, I thought it was best to be open to all sorts of new areas. I didn't intend to complete my studies, I just thought I'd bide my time until I knew what I wanted to do. I never could have envisioned what was about to happen to me. Imagine starting a successful cosmetics business at age eighteen!

I started wearing makeup at the age of sixteen, trying to look older than I was. My mother wore her makeup in a very distinctive fashion, similar to that of women in the 1920s and 1930s—dark, smokey eyes; pale skin; and deep, rich lipstick. I really liked this look

and tried to copy it, but it was hard for me to find m.
instead of glossy or frosted kinds. It was also hard to find l.
deep reds and browns. I knew you could get these kinds of li.
overseas because that's where my mother had found them, but t.
weren't available in Australia.

It was obvious to me that there was a gap in the market. I didn't
need the IQ of a genius to figure this out, especially when I would
ask salespeople at cosmetics counters for the products I wanted.
They would respond, "If I only had a dollar for every time someone
asked for that. . . ." I began to think, "Imagine if I had ten dollars
every time someone asked for a matte lipstick."

At this stage, the business was just the seed of an idea. I was
young, and I had no way of financing such a venture. My family
wasn't wealthy, so I couldn't borrow the money from them. A bank
would have laughed at me if I asked for a loan. It hadn't occurred to
me to raise the money myself—until one very important day.

About halfway through my first year at the university, I was
sitting at home reading a magazine when I came across an ad for an
award offered to five people under age twenty-one. The award was
twenty thousand dollars to get an idea off the ground. It could be
an idea for a business, for an art project, or for the community. The
second I saw that ad, I went from being a consumer to being an
entrepreneur. If I was a cartoon character, a lightbulb would have
appeared above my head. I decided to apply for the award and to
start a business selling matte lipsticks.

I began to research Australia's cosmetics manufacturing industry.
I made some calls and found several contract cosmetics chemists
who could manufacture my product. I also found people who could
provide the packaging. I put together a broad business plan and
sent it off, keeping my fingers crossed. I didn't get the award, but
now that I'd learned it was possible to manufacture lipstick in
Australia, I was determined to do so.

I began to think of other ways I could finance my business. As
I was exploring different possibilities, something happened that I
can only describe as a modern-day fairy tale. I went to a party one
night and bumped into a friend of mine whom I hadn't seen in a
while. I was telling her about my business idea, and she suggested

I contact a friend of hers whose father was a successful business-man in Melbourne. She said he might be able to give me some advice. I didn't follow through on this, but a couple of weeks later, he called me and asked to hear about my idea. He said he had some capital (money he had saved for investing later) and was interested in starting a business.

I met with him and convinced him of the potential my idea had. He didn't know a lot about the cosmetics market but was impressed with my confidence. He talked to some of his female friends about my idea, and they said they would buy matte lipsticks if they were available. He and I officially became business partners.

We spent the first two months getting all of the major financial pieces of the puzzle in place. He then went on to begin a new career as a lawyer, and I worked on the business full-time. I met with him regularly to get advice and to keep him up-to-date.

For most of that year, I worked with the chemists to formulate the product. I didn't have a background in chemistry, so I just directed them and explained what I wanted. I wanted the matte lip-stick to be long-lasting and intense. I showed them the colors I was looking for, using paint chips and fabric swatches as examples. They mixed up many different samples for me to try. After about eight months, I felt that the product was ready.

At the same time that I was working with the chemists, I was also getting everything else ready to go. I'd been working with a graphic artist on the packaging and display of the product. I was my own test market, so I thought about how I would want the product presented if I was the customer. I wanted the packaging to be bold and differ-ent, yet feminine and elegant. I always knew I wanted the brand to be called Poppy—not because it's my name but because I love the image the poppy flower evokes. I also knew I wanted the logo to be black and red.

I started to think about where I wanted to sell my products. I decided to approach fashion boutiques instead of department stores and drugstores because I wanted the lipsticks to be more of a fashion accessory than a cosmetic. This idea was unique because in Australia makeup wasn't usually sold in fashion stores.

Before my product was ready to sell, I made an appointment with Australian *Vogue* magazine. They decided to do a small story about my business and, as luck would have it, the issue came out during the month I began selling my lipsticks.

One of the last things I needed to do before my product went to market was to name each lipstick. I wanted to do this instead of just giving each one a number. I felt that everything about my lipsticks was unique, and I wanted their names to be unique, too. To me, the names of many lipsticks on the market ("Tangerine Dream," for example) seemed too old-fashioned and sappy in a world where women are lawyers, doctors, politicians, and business owners. I named my first line of colors "Ambition," "Liberty," "Inspiration," "Courage," "Unity," "Virtue," and "Integrity."

Poppy lipsticks

Because my first line of colors consisted of seven lipsticks, I wanted to launch other lines of seven colors. I began thinking about names of things that came in sevens: the Seven Wonders of the World (too grandiose), the seven days of the week (cute, but not right), the Seven Dwarfs (definitely not right!). Then I thought of the Seven Deadly Sins, which seemed like great names for lipsticks. It's fun to watch customers choosing between "Envy" or "Integrity."

When my first line of lipsticks went on sale, the business went bang! I received about fifty calls a day from people who wanted to buy my products. By the end of the third month, the largest department store chain in the country was stocking my lipsticks. The business had recovered its forty thousand dollars in start-up costs and was already making a profit.

Soon after, I decided to buy out my business partner and run the business myself. By this time, I was twenty years old. We negotiated and eventually settled on a price. I asked my brother, Justin, to join me as codirector.

Next, I decided to go to New York City to begin to get a sense of the international marketplace. I came across a store called Barney's, which I thought would be perfect for my products. I called the store's buyer and, fortunately, got an appointment the next day. She loved the product and decided to launch it the following year in their new Madison Avenue store.

The line has been a great success in the United States. Some weeks it outsells many well-established, multinational brands of lipstick. I have now released three other lines of lipstick.

My brother and I have a big dream and are willing to risk everything for it. Right now, we're working to grow the business to a higher level, which involves a major financial commitment. I see the business as a ship: The ship we're sailing at the moment is fine for the seas we're in, but if we were to go to greater seas in the same ship, cracks would form and we'd eventually sink.

People often ask me about the difficulties I've faced in starting a business, but the truth is that setting up was the easy part compared to what I'm doing now. The greatest challenge is to keep the momentum.

Danyel Bell

The Cheesecake Lady

Seventeen-year-old Danyel Bell is from Lawrence, Kansas. She lives with her parents, Douglas and Mildred, and her nine brothers and sisters. Danyel's father runs his own equipment rental business, and her mother is a homemaker.

Danyel loves school, especially business and math classes. She hopes to someday attend General Motors Engineering and Management Institute, and to major in computer engineering and business management. Danyel is the senior class vice president of the Lawrence chapter of the Distributive Education Clubs of America (DECA) and a member of the National Honor Society. She works as a filing clerk for an insurance agency and as a salesperson in a locally owned interior decorating store (in addition to running her own business). Danyel is always ready for new responsibilities, and she's never afraid to take chances.

I STARTED MY CHEESECAKE BUSINESS IN THE EIGHTH GRADE. I GAVE A woman who worked as a custodian at my school one of the first cheesecakes I made. She told me that she really liked it. A little later, she came back and asked me how much I'd charge to make another cheesecake. I received five dollars to make a plain one.

That summer, I had the opportunity to take a driver's education course, which cost eighty dollars. My parents agreed to pay for half of the fee if I would pay for the rest. An eye exam was also required, which cost an additional forty dollars. I decided to try to sell my cheesecakes to make money to pay for driver's education. By the time I had finished selling the cakes, I was able to pay the entire enrollment fee. My parents paid for my eye exam.

I now sell plain cheesecakes for six dollars and cherry cheesecakes for nine dollars. I've recently started making strawberry ones, too. My customers are primarily the faculty of the school I attend, my peers, and their parents. I don't think that I'm doing some great thing. People often ask me if I intend to take this business venture to a new level once I graduate from high school, and I honestly don't know. Right now, I like the fact that I have to prove myself to people and promote my product.

Currently, I'm taking my first marketing class. Because of my experience with my business and various other seminars I've attended, the concepts in the class aren't that difficult for me. I've learned that the best form of advertising is by word-of-mouth, but I knew that before I started taking the class. Word-of-mouth has been a great way to sell my cheesecakes.

Danyel Bell

With this business, I'm making my mark. People trust me and recognize who I am. My greatest support has been my family. My parents let me use their oven free of charge when I have a cheesecake order. If I don't feel well, my two younger sisters bake the cheesecakes for me because I don't have any employees. Of course, I split the profits with them.

In my business, I don't make an incredible amount of money, but because my business expenses are so low (I only have to buy ingredients), I usually make more than a 50 percent profit. I put some of the money back into the business, save part of it, and use the rest for personal expenses.

This business has taught me to finish whatever I start. Many of my customers come to me because they plan to have company and, with their busy schedules, they don't have time to prepare a delicious homemade dessert. When I say, "Place an order one day, and it will be delivered the next," my customers believe me, and they depend on me to follow through. Often, my customers like to take one of my cheesecakes to functions so they can say *they* made it—but other people there usually know it's not true. I like knowing that people love my product.

There are several things I would recommend about starting a business. First, you have to give people a reason to trust you before they'll buy something from you, so be honest and professional. Attend business seminars and try networking (meeting with others for information and advice). Networking has allowed me to meet many interesting people and to move my business forward. Also, be aware of your market—some people might not find your product useful. Concentrate on winning customers who truly have a need for your product.

I've learned never to be afraid to get advice about what to do next. I really appreciate the small business development center in my community. I've gotten to know the director, and she's helped me by telling me about upcoming seminars.

If you have a dream that you think can become a reality, give it a try. Remember to check out all of your options before jumping into a business venture, and always leave a safety net. Statistics show that many businesses fail after the first two years, often because the owner isn't good at handling the finances. Most of all, pace yourself. Don't try to progress too quickly. Enjoy every moment!

The very best advice I can give about becoming an entrepreneur is: Have fun with what you do. Often, running your own business means working more than eight hours a day. It's important to enjoy your work and make the most of it. You must be confident, believe that you have a product that can help people, and do everything in your power to prove it.

K-K Gregory

Wristies, Inc.

Thirteen-year-old K-K Gregory of Bedford, Massachusetts, was recently one of twelve young people to be inducted into the Kids' Hall of Fame in Washington, D.C. She is the youngest person ever to be nominated as Entrepreneur of the Year in the New England division. K-K enjoys math, playing the keyboard, and getting together with her friends in her free time. She has been active in gymnastics for eight years. During the summer, she attends Camp Newfound in Maine, where she has received the Gold Star camper award.

K-K's parents are Susan, a seamstress, and Scott, who works for Kodak. K-K has one brother, ten-year-old Colby, who likes to play soccer. The family has a white cat named Snowball.

ONE DAY, THERE WAS A BIG SNOWSTORM IN MY TOWN, AND THAT night I went outside to build a fort with my younger brother. While we were working on the fort, my wrists started bothering me. It was getting really dark outside, and my mom came out and asked us how we were doing. She said, "Look at you! You have snow all over your mittens and halfway up your sleeves. Why don't you go in and sew something to fix that?"

I went inside and asked my mom to sew two tubes out of a fabric called Polartec to fit over my wrists. After she had made the tubes for me, I placed them on my wrists. I then realized that I needed to be able to hook the fabric onto my hands to keep it in place. I made a hole in each tube so my thumbs could poke through. The first time I tested the tubes, I placed them over my gloves, but I found that snow piled up around my palms. This made it hard to play and to build

K-K Gregory

things. I went back inside and asked my mom to make the tubes smaller to fit *under* my gloves. I tried them, and THEY WORKED!

A few weeks later, my Girl Scout troop had a snow party to earn a badge called "Outdoor Fun." I made pairs of the fabric tubes for everybody in my troop, and they said, "Oh yes! I'm so glad I got a pair. I really need these!" All of the girls tried them at the party, and the following day at school they told me that the wrist protectors really worked. Their wrists stayed dry and warm, and snow didn't go up their sleeves. They also told me that I should enter my invention into a contest.

I decided to contact my friend's father, who's an inventor, and he told me to call his patent attorney. A patent* is a right that the government grants you to prevent other people from manufacturing,

---

*To learn more about patents, see p. 144.

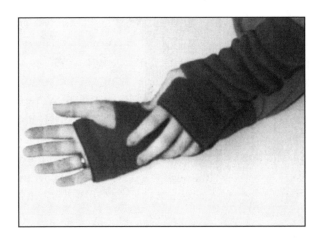

Wristies fit over
the thumb and
palm, and slide
over the wrist.

using, or selling your invention for a certain number of years. It's a
good way to protect your invention. When I met with the patent
attorney, I showed him my wrist protectors and he thought they were
a great idea.

My mom and I did a lot of research about gloves and mittens to
see if anyone else already had a product similar to mine. We looked
at encyclopedias and reference books, and we found that no one had
yet invented wrist protectors like the ones I created. We then worked
with the attorney and applied for a patent.

Next, we made up a name for my product, Wristies, and applied
for a trademark (a trademark identifies your product).* This was the
start of my business!

Wristies are selling really well. In fact, Wristies, Inc., signed a
license and sale agreement with the Turtle Fur company to sell
Wristies to the winter sporting goods industry. Wristies is now a
registered trademark, and you can find my products in ski stores.

During the winter of 1995, several exciting things happened with
Wristies. I was interviewed on TV, and after the interview I received
more than 250 calls. I instantly had to start a mail-order business and
get another phone line.

Since then, Wristies have been mailed to customers in places like
Alaska, Colorado, Delaware, and Italy. McDonald's restaurants ordered

---

*To learn more about trademarks, see p. 144.

Wristies by the hundreds for their drive-through workers. Members of the design department of WGBH Channel 2, a Boston public television station, wear Wristies while they work on their computers.

In addition, workers at Malden Mills, where I buy the fabric for Wristies, wore my product while they were rebuilding their mills after a fire. I donated Wristies to the workers to show my appreciation for the fabric they make and to support them as they rebuilt their company. The president of Malden Mills, Aaron Feuerstein, met with me and thanked me personally for my donation. On the way home from the meeting, I said, "I'm so happy! I met my role model! I want my company to be just like his."

I was the invited speaker at Take Our Daughters to Work Day in April of 1996 in Boston. That summer, other exciting things happened. I learned that Wristies would be offered in Brookstone's Hard-to-Find Tools catalog, along with a small story about the origin of Wristies. Also, *National Geographic World* magazine wanted to feature me in an issue.

K-K with Wristies

Some of my customers include people who have disabilities, arthritis, or carpal tunnel syndrome. Other people who wear Wristies are snow shovelers, skiers, sledders, runners, typists, gas station attendants, delivery people, drivers, garbage collectors, law enforcement officers, postal carriers, people who can't find gloves that fit, children who hate gloves and mittens, dancers, band players, pianists, bulldozer operators, bicyclists, and people who repair clock towers. Many of these people wear Wristies to keep warm, even in the house! Others wear them for wrist support.

Some people who have encouraged me along the way are Mr. Feuerstein, who gave me confidence, and other inventors, who offered helpful hints. My mom has been the most help, doing things when I'm busy and also interpreting the paperwork that's too complicated for me. Two long-term goals I have are to earn one million dollars and to retire by age forty.

Running my business has been very exciting. But if you're thinking of starting a business of your own, be very ready for a lot of work. Find people who believe in your idea and GO FOR IT!

Mindy Ann Nunez

M.A.N. Designs

Mindy Ann Nunez, age seventeen, is a junior at a Catholic high school in St. Bernard parish outside of New Orleans, Louisiana. She lives with her parents, Marc and Cheryl, who are co-owners of an auto parts store. Mindy has a twenty-four-year-old sister named Nicole.

Mindy belongs to many school clubs, including Mu Alpha Theta, National Honor Society, the admissions team, peer facilitators, the foreign language club, and the science club. She's also the secretary of the student council. Mindy has been on the cross-country team since eighth grade and is a three-year lettered athlete in the sport. She's also a varsity letterholder on the track team. Mindy is consistently on the high honor roll in academics, and her favorite subjects are history, psychology, and English. She has received a partial academic scholarship to her high school.

M<small>Y STORY BEGINS IN 1995, WHEN</small> I <small>BEGAN WORKING FOR A LOCAL</small> bakery. I worked there for about six months with five or six other girls, who were all making the same minimum wage salary as I was. At the time, my father was selling automotive decals at his store as a favor for a boy he knew. The shiny decals were made from vinyl, with an adhesive on the back, and they featured cartoon characters, words, or familiar logos. People put the decals on the windows of their cars or trucks, and my dad noticed that the stickers were in hot demand.

At work, the sweet smell of doughnuts made me feel ill every time I walked into the bakery. It wasn't that the doughnuts were bad, I was just sick of them! So when my dad came up with the idea to set up a vinyl decal shop in our home, I quickly agreed to run it, and M.A.N. Designs was born.

My family and I went into this business with a very limited knowledge of it. We learned most of the basics from our family friend, Glen, who works with computers during the day and surfs the Internet at night. The decals, he told us, were cut from a machine that runs from a computer. Glen found a dealer who could sell this kind of machine to me. We already had a home computer, which I knew how to use pretty well. I borrowed money from my parents to purchase the new software, which Glen loaded onto our computer.

A week of trial and error followed, with Glen trying to learn the new software and teach it to me. He figured out that we needed another piece of equipment—a scanner. It was a very stressful time, but once we finally got everything going, running the software was a piece of cake. I began making and selling decals and earning money. I eventually quit working at the bakery, and now I work at M.A.N. Designs after school and on weekends.

Mindy Ann Nunez

Running a business has turned out to be a priceless learning experience. I've really grown up, and I now appreciate things I might otherwise have taken for granted. For example, I've learned that time is invaluable and that good time-management skills can be one of your greatest assets. I have to set my own hours at M.A.N. Designs, which means I have to find the motivation to go to work when I'm at home, instead of lounging around or surfing the World Wide Web. With such a busy schedule, time has become very precious to me.

I'm also learning the benefits of being a hard worker. The harder I work, the more money M.A.N. Designs makes. On the other hand, if I don't work, the business doesn't earn money. While my friends are begging for and borrowing money to go out on the weekends, I usually have a nice stash of cash. I buy my own clothes and my own everyday things like lunch, gasoline, and cosmetics. I've also been able to save quite a lot of money in the bank for college and a new car.

My business attracts customers by word-of-mouth. I don't advertise in the traditional ways because this would probably bring too much business, and I'm busy enough as it is! I feel blessed that, for the most part, M.A.N. Designs has been financially successful. The

Mindy at M.A.N. Designs

money that I borrowed from my parents, used initially as capital, has been repaid. Since then, I've borrowed again to upgrade my software, and I'm paying that money back in monthly installments. M.A.N. Designs has its own checking account, and I now have a nice investment in computer equipment and software. I've also gained experience that you can't put a price tag on.

Because the demand for vinyl decals has slowed down, M.A.N. Designs has begun to take a different route. I've started focusing on signs and lettering instead of just decals. Although the decals still sell quite well, I'm considering moving into the competitive field of advertising and sign making. With little local competition, this field looks very promising.

My own high school has done a lot of business with me. I do annual "drug-free" signs for the guidance department, as well as all of the lettering for the drama department's theater posters. I also make the cheerleaders' spirit signs. I'm currently exploring the fields of screen-printing and making transfers for T-shirts.

I think the future of my business is solid while I'm in high school, but it becomes uncertain after that. I have to decide whether I want to continue running the business while I'm in college. I might go to college in another state and take my business with me, or I might choose a college that's near home so I can keep the business here.

I would definitely encourage other teenagers to become entrepreneurs. The benefits of owning your own business are countless. I would, however, like to give some advice to enterprising teens. The first thing is that it helps to have the support of your parents. If they think that your idea might not be realistic or that your product won't sell well, they could be right. Your parents may know more about the economic situation of your town or city, so get some advice from them or from other people you trust.

Also, it helps to have access to someone who knows how to do the bookkeeping for your business, or someone who can show you how to do it yourself. Taxes can be very confusing!

And finally, have fun! I know that one of the biggest problems I have is worrying too much about my business. I'm getting better about this, though, and I'm learning that even if the business fails, it still will have been a great learning experience. So get moving already!

Jeanie and Elizabeth Low

J & E Innovations

Jeanie Low, age fourteen, and her sister, Elizabeth, age eleven, are inventors. The sisters are recognized as two of the youngest females with U.S. patents. In May of 1996, the two of them were inducted into the International Hall of Fame as Student Inventors of the Year.

The Low sisters live in Houston, Texas, with their dad, Richard, who's a pediatrician, and their mom, Susan, who manages their father's office. The girls have two brothers, William and Christensen, as well as a hamster named Samson, a cat named Cindy, and a dog named Lady.

Jeanie is a ninth grader at Michael DeBakey School for Health Professions, where she's an honor student and enjoys science. Jeanie also likes horseback riding, ice-skating, and playing with her pets. Elizabeth, a sixth grader at Paul Revere Middle School, is in the honors program at school. She rides horses (English, western, and bareback styles), and she enjoys roller skating, ice-skating, and playing with her animals. The two sisters are part of a close-knit family and enjoy going on fun trips together.

JEANIE: ABOUT NINE YEARS AGO, I INVENTED THE KIDDIE STOOL, A folding stool that attaches to the outside of a cabinet. When the stool is needed, you can pull it down from the cabinet door. Then you can simply fold it up when you're done, conserving valuable household space. The stool was designed for young children so they could reach the bathroom sink.

Jeanie Low

My father was the inspiration for the Kiddie Stool—he's the inspiration for all of my inventions. The Kiddie Stool won first place at the annual Houston Invention Association fair, which was the first time I showed my invention in public. I never would have thought that nine years later my invention would be such a success. I patented the Kiddie Stool to protect it, and I've received a registered trademark to identify my product.* I've also exhibited the Kiddie Stool at many national shows, appeared on local TV programs, been the subject of newspaper and magazine articles, and have spoken before the Houston Chamber of Commerce, the Houston Invention Society, and the Texas Creative Society. I was even flown out to Hollywood to do a national television show called *Why Didn't I Think of That?*

---

*To learn more about patents and trademarks, see p. 144.

Now my sister, Elizabeth, and I have our own company, called J & E Innovations, to market our inventions and to talk to other students about how to invent and market new products. Any profits we earn are equally split between Elizabeth and me. We've had real board meetings, and we've issued stock and quarterly reports. Our reports release financial information about our company.

As a representative of the company, I've done many exciting things. For example, my father and I completed an infomercial on inventing, and my sister and I made a CD-ROM for the Discovery Channel. We've also been featured in two books. It's been a long journey for us. Along the way, we've met a lot of interesting people and have made many new friends.

Creating inventions and starting a business have allowed me to use my imagination and to succeed. When I get older, I hope to pursue a career in marketing or in medicine. If I were to give any advice to some-

**Jeanie with the
Kiddie Stool**

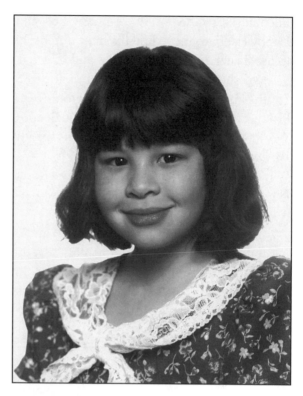

Elizabeth Low

one starting a business, I'd say to make sure your product is unique. Checking the originality of your product is an important step before starting a company, seeking a patent, or registering for a trademark.

ELIZABETH: I'VE JUST RETURNED FROM BOSTON, WHERE I'VE BEEN inspecting the final stages of production on my invention, Happy Hand—a fun paperweight made from surgical gloves and sand. You can form the fingers into shapes to hold a business card, a pen, or jewelry. The fingers will stay in any pose you want, and you can paint the hands in your favorite colors and designs. While in Boston, I signed a contract between a local company and J & E Innovations to start making the Happy Hand. After years of effort, it looks like all of my work is finally paying off.

I came up with the idea for the Happy Hand when I was only four years old. I entered the invention in the Houston Invention Society Exhibit and, to my surprise, won first place against students in elementary school and high school. I even got to be on TV.

Encouraged by the positive response, I began to experiment with the Happy Hand, trying to find the most durable kinds of sand and gloves to use. I later applied for a patent and received one in March of 1994.

I've shown the Happy Hand at the U.S. Patent Show at the Smithsonian Institution in Washington, D.C., at the Inventing New Products Exposition (INPEX), and at Epcot Center at Walt Disney World in Florida. Articles about my product have appeared in *Woman's Day* and the *Washington Post*. I've been on the TV show *Why Didn't I Think of That?* with my sister, and I even sold two Happy Hands to Thing the Actor, whose hand plays "Thing" in the Addams Family movies.

In order to market the Happy Hand and other products, my sister and I decided to go into business together. We needed a good name for our company, so we settled on J & E Innovations. We liked the word "Innovations" because it says "new ideas" and "the future." We did research to see if that name was already taken (it

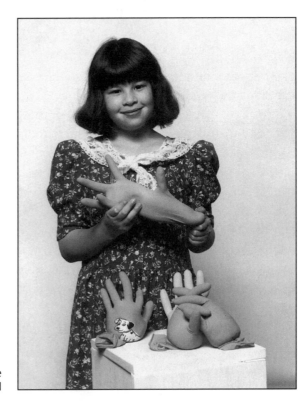

**Elizabeth with the
Happy Hand**

wasn't), and we created a business plan. Then we went to the Secretary of State in Texas to form the company. We were granted a charter to do business in the state of Texas.

In 1996, I applied for a trademark for the name Happy Hand. The trademark was granted, and the name Happy Hand was placed on the public register. With the patent and trademark granted, I was ready to sell my product.

My sister and I began to talk to Bob Wilson and Jerry Joy of J & W Enterprises about producing and marketing the Happy Hand. We had first met Bob and Jerry at the U.S. Patent Show. Their company, located in Boston, has the machinery to manufacture the Happy Hand. We negotiated a contract with J & W Enterprises over several months. After many versions of the contract had been sent back and forth, we decided to meet in person at the Boston factory to officially sign the contract. While in Boston, Jeanie and I were interviewed by the *Boston Globe*. We also took a tour of the factory to see how the Happy Hand was made.

To produce a Happy Hand, special sand is weighed and sifted, then put into the glove by a machine. The Hands are secured by a plastic clasp or are tied by hand like a balloon. The packages for Happy Hands are see-through so customers know what they're buying. Each package has bright, eye-catching colors and features lots of information about the product and about me. The logo is yellow and red, with the words "Happy Hand" surrounding a smiley face.

Producing the Happy Hand is a continuous learning experience. As production has expanded, we've run into problems that we've had to fix. A new way to tie the hands was developed, for example. And a vacuum hose is now used to suck the air out of the gloves before packaging them.

We've done several promotional appearances to help market the Happy Hand. Many different types of stores now distribute the product. After so much hard work, it's been very exciting to see the Happy Hand in stores!

Jeanie and Elizabeth Low's Top Ten List for Starting a Successful Company

1. Talk with other people who have started companies from scratch. Get their ideas and help.

2. Find out your state's laws on how to set up a company. Each state's laws are different.

3. Keep the company's name short and easy to pronounce (for example, J & E).

4. Make the company's name broad enough to cover new products. For example: If your company's name is Joe's Pizza, you couldn't just start selling chicken without first changing the name.

5. Create a business plan that outlines what you hope to accomplish with your company.

6. Follow through with what you start. It takes time to develop ideas and to get a company off the ground, so don't get discouraged too fast.

7. When designing your company's products, use a colorful logo and fun packaging.

8. If you have more than one product, you might want to incorporate (form into a legal corporation). Make sure you research the process of incorporation, with help from a librarian, lawyer, or other professional.

9. Protect your product with a patent and protect the name with a trademark.

10. *Above all, have fun with your products and company!*

Angélica Marie Rivera-Cabañas

Destiny

Seventeen-year-old Angélica Marie Rivera-Cabañas is from San Juan, Puerto Rico. She's the fifth of eight daughters born to her parents, Juan and Ilka Rivera, and she has an identical twin sister named Amanda. Angélica attends a private school, Wesleyan Academy, where she enjoys studying English, biology, and pre-calculus. Her jewelry business helps her to pay for tuition and school expenses. In her free time, she enjoys playing softball, singing, writing, and publishing poetry on the Internet. Angélica is an active member of her community, caring for the elderly at a nursing home, babysitting, and tutoring young children in her neighborhood.

AT THE AGE OF THIRTEEN, I ENCOUNTERED MANY CHALLENGES. My father owned a company that distributed Rainbow vacuum cleaners, and he had four offices on the island of Puerto Rico. During the Persian Gulf War, his business dropped dramatically, and he was forced to declare bankruptcy. As one of eight children, I was faced with the dilemma of not knowing whether my family would still be able to live in our neighborhood, or if the next day we would lose everything.

This economic hardship brought other consequences as well. My father could no longer afford to pay for our private school tuition. But I didn't let this situation hamper my hopes of staying in the school I loved. I decided to take matters into my own hands.

I began to look for work options that would allow me to pay for my studies. I searched in the newspaper, and I also contacted my friends and relatives. I eventually purchased silver jewelry from a wholesaler (one who sells in quantity for resale). I was able to buy the jewelry using money that I had borrowed from my dad and earned from babysitting. I planned to resell the silver jewelry for a profit.

As soon as I had made my first purchase, I started selling the jewelry. I carried it around school in a cookie box. After I sold all of this merchandise, I was happy with the results. I earned so much money that I was able to pay my father back and to have some money left for the next jewelry purchase. I never thought that an eighth grader could have hundreds of dollars in a piggy bank!

Thanks to my business, I was able to pay for my private school tuition and other expenses. Since then, I've successfully continued to buy and sell silver jewelry. Every weekend, I visit different

**Angélica Marie
Rivera-Cabañas**

wholesalers in Old San Juan, and I invest part of my earnings in new merchandise. My goal for each week is to sell at least 25 percent more than the previous week.

Because of the rapid growth of my business, I was forced to buy new equipment. I invested in a large display case, which I carry with me at all times so I can show new products to regular customers—my classmates, the members of my church, and my neighbors. In order to better market my jewelry, I offer special discounts ranging from 20 to 40 percent off to my frequent customers, as well as to customers who place multiple orders. I also distribute my business cards in the community to create name recognition and to gain the attention of prospective customers.

I've had very positive results from my business, but I've also experienced difficulties. After the first few years, my business slowed down a little because I ran out of customers. Instead of giving up, I opted to enter into a partnership with my twin sister and one of my friends. After we'd formed the partnership, we began to sell jewelry in my friend's neighborhood. Each one of us went through the neighborhood and sold jewelry door-to-door. This business venture worked out well for a while, but our earnings had to be divided among the three of us, which made it harder for me to earn the amount of money I needed to cover my tuition. When my friends decided to drop out of the business, I began selling jewelry on my own again.

Experiences like this have made owning a business the greatest achievement of my life. I've grown mentally and emotionally. I've learned that everything I want to do, no matter how big or how small, becomes possible if I do it with all my heart and all my will. I've learned to be successful in everything I do and to manage my time in a way that allows me to devote time to my business, keep up with my studies and school activities, and still have time to volunteer in my community.

My short-term goal is to have my own jewelry store in a mall where I can sell the finest silver jewelry, including pieces imported from Mexico and from fine crafters around the world. I also intend to design and create my own jewelry line. Besides selling jewelry, I'd

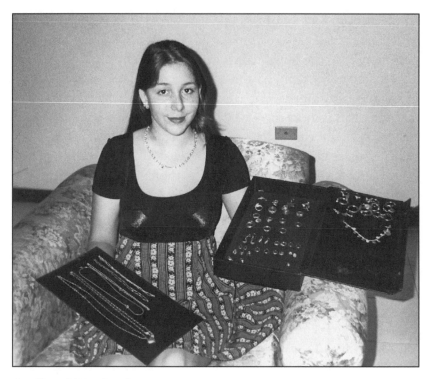

Angélica with her jewelry

like to have a small section in my store devoted to selling greeting cards with my poetry on them. This way, customers can purchase the cards to accompany the silver jewelry if they intend to buy my jewelry as a gift. With the money I'm earning from my business, I hope to continue paying for my studies, which will help me to accomplish my long-term goal.

My long-term goal is to further my education after graduating from high school. Because of my love for working with the public on a daily basis, I'd like to continue my studies in the area of entrepreneurship. I'd also like to study law so that I can help those who are often forgotten in our community. By becoming a civil rights lawyer, I hope to fight for the rights of people with disabilities, children, and those who've been denied their rights based on race. At the same time, I hope to continue to run my small business.

Thanks to the support of my family, I've had the opportunity to learn firsthand that my goals aren't far-fetched. I was able to attend Camp Entrepreneur at the National Educational Center for Women in Business held at Seton Hill College in Greensburg, Pennsylvania. Those who attended included other young women from various parts of the U.S. who already owned their own businesses or had the desire to do so one day. I met businesswomen who not only served as an inspiration to me but also offered some helpful hints about developing, owning, and successfully managing a business. At the camp seminars I attended, I learned about a budget and an income, how to save money for my business, and how to pay myself for the work I do. After attending this camp, I realized that I can be successful as both a lawyer and a small-business owner.

My advice to young entrepreneurs like myself is to believe that everything in life is possible. You can succeed in everything you do. Always, always work to achieve your goals. Move forward with every step you make. Never, never step back. Reach out for new ideas to keep your business running smoothly. Be positive even if you encounter a negative situation. After all, everything in life has a purpose. Maybe the negative situation will help you to learn and grow.

Girl Scout Troop 278

Madame Mimm's Workshop

The members of Girl Scout troop 278 in Gainesville, Florida, are Allison Cullinan, Keely Fielding, Holly Gershow, Lauren Gossinger, Sarah Katherine Harrington, Alyssa Krop, Mala Kay Lawrence, Summer Lloyd-Turner, Christina Puntervold, Julie Rosselle, and Courtenay Staples. They are all in ninth grade and attend five different high schools.

The girls have diverse interests and are all involved in many different extracurricular activities, such as volunteering, horseback riding, swim team, piano, dance, cheerleading, volleyball, and drama. One thing they all hold in common is their commitment—to the Girl Scouts and to their business of selling arts and crafts. The troop members believe that Madame Mimm's Workshop has been a valuable learning experience. Although they don't know what the future holds for them, the girls feel confident that the entrepreneurial skills they've learned will help them in any other business ventures or challenges in life.

OUR ARTS AND CRAFTS BUSINESS IS CALLED MADAME MIMM'S Workshop. We came up with this name because we wanted something that sounded magical. Many of our craft items reflect a make-believe, fairy-tale quality.

The business began as a way to fund scouting field trips that our parents weren't willing or able to finance. We started learning about budgets and decided to hold a garage sale to earn money for the trips we wanted to take. The first garage sale was a big success, and

Girl Scout troop 278. *From left to right, standing:* **Allison, Summer, Holly, Christina, Sarah, Mala Kay, and Alyssa.** *From left to right, sitting:* **Keely, Courtenay, and Lauren.**

we were able to use the money we earned to travel to Savannah, Georgia, where we visited the home of the founder of Girl Scouts in the United States, Juliette Lowe.

A year went by, and we held another garage sale to finance another trip. We then went to Charleston, South Carolina, to stay overnight on a ship called the *U.S.S. Yorktown* and to explore the area around the old slave market.

When we started middle school, we set higher goals for ourselves. Realizing that arts and crafts fairs were becoming more popular, we decided to join the crafts scene. All of us had learned arts and crafts both at school and in Girl Scouts, so we felt confident that we could make and sell our own goods at shows.

The first year, we brainstormed ideas and tried many craft items. We decided that the key to success was to keep our costs down and our prices low. We felt a little nervous because we were twelve- and thirteen-year-olds competing with adult artists who had years of experience at arts and crafts shows. Because most of the big shows charged an enormous fee to enter, and because of our previous success with garage sales, we decided to hold an arts and crafts sale of our own. We joined with a troop that had more experience in craft shows so we could learn what to do.

The show was a real learning experience for all of the troop members and for our leaders. We found that everyone who came to our show loved our crafts and spent quite a bit of money. Although the event wasn't as well attended as we'd hoped, we felt encouraged by the money we earned. Our profit was almost 25 percent more than the profits earned from our garage sales, even taking into account our labor and the cost of materials.

The following year, we held our own arts and crafts show again. This time, we planned it for the same weekend as Gainesville's Fall Festival and Craft Fair. We held our show closer to the area of the big fair so we could attract more customers. But we were still somewhat disappointed by the attendance. Although our second event generated more sales, it seemed as if people really weren't taking us seriously.

The second show did have benefits, though. It proved to us that we were beginning to understand what people wanted to buy and what we were able to produce. We talked it over afterwards and decided to enter a big craft show. After all, once people saw our merchandise, they usually bought it. The problem was getting enough people to attend.

The following spring, a lucky thing happened. We found out that we could enter Gainesville's Spring Arts Festival as young artists and not have to pay an entrance fee. We were eager to expand our business because we wanted to travel overseas to visit Pax Lodge, a Girl Scout World Center in London, England—one of the four Girl Scout centers in the world. We needed to earn more money to take the trip.

The Spring Arts Festival was held during the weekend of our spring break. Because many of our troop members planned to be out of town with their families that weekend, we decided that the girls who were able to attend the festival would sell their goods as individuals and keep the profits for themselves. That way, some of us would earn spending money for London. Plus the spring show would help us to determine which craft products our customers liked most. Knowing what our customers were looking for would help us at sales held the following fall.

The Spring Arts Festival turned out to be a marketing bonanza for us! We'd been concentrating on Christmas ornaments, flowerpots, and jewelry—items that mostly appealed to adults. But at this festival, we added some items especially for children, and we learned that our real skill was making things for young people. After all, it hadn't been that long since we were little kids ourselves, and we certainly were experts on what little girls liked! Some of our most popular items were barrettes and jewelry, ballerina bunnies and bears, and halo garlands made from wire and covered with glitter.

By this time, we had also begun to host children's parties, since we were good at making party favors and knew a lot of games. Hosting parties became an important new part of our business. The craft shows and parties took a lot of time, but there was a big reward. In February, our troop and our leaders flew to London and spent a

Madame Mimm's Workshop

week at Pax Lodge. All but one girl made the trip, and we all agreed that our hard work had been worth it.

Now that we're in high school, we find it more difficult to meet and to find time to make our products, but we're persevering. We continue to introduce new products at our shows to attract new customers and to keep our business fresh and creative. We haven't yet decided on our next travel destination, but we know we want to go overseas. It will probably take more than a year for us to earn enough money to reach this goal. If we continue working hard at Madame Mimm's Workshop, we'll succeed.

We feel that Troop 278 isn't your average Girl Scout troop. We have high goals and put in a lot of extra work to make Madame Mimm's Workshop succeed. We accept each other's differences, and we value each other's strengths. For example, some of us are better at selling and marketing than production. Some of us are good at creating displays and advertising our products. A few of us are truly gifted craftspeople and artists. Combining our talents and working together has helped our business to become a financial success.

After three years of making and selling our own arts and crafts, we've made great strides. When the date of each show approaches, we all pitch in to get the work accomplished. We've learned that cooperation is an important part of running a strong business.

The best piece of advice we can give to other entrepreneurs is: Don't be afraid of hard work or taking risks. Keep trying no matter what obstacles you encounter. Persistence can bring great rewards!

Product Businesses

Questions to Think About, Ideas to Try

1. What products would you like to see on the market, and which existing products would you like to improve? Survey your family, friends, and other people of all ages for their ideas. This is a great way to start a list of potential products for your business.

2. Manufacturing products can be expensive. What steps do you need to take to produce quality products at the lowest possible cost? Make a chart to record your material costs, your labor costs, and the estimated selling or retail price of your product. Determine if your business will actually make a profit. If it doesn't look profitable, find ways to cut costs or to increase the price of your product.

3. Marketing strategies are vital to the owner of any type of business. How will you market your product? Determine the type of marketing that's best for your business (newspaper, radio, or television; flyers; word-of-mouth; etc.). What can you afford to use? What will reach your customers? Which strategy will give you the most customers for your money?

4. Brainstorm a list of unconventional marketing strategies. To help you with this process, think of places where people frequently go (grocery stores, parking lots, banks, etc.). Could you advertise at one of these places? Where do people have to stand in line—how can you capture their attention while they wait? Think of other ways your message could be delivered (through song? on the World Wide Web? through skits?).

5. Start a Young Entrepreneurs Club for the youth in your community. Your local chamber of commerce, small business owners, the mayor, banks, etc., may want to assist by collaborating with you. Write down your club's goals and objectives. How will you attract members? What activities will the club provide? Could local business owners offer presentations to your club members?

6. Jeanie and Elizabeth Low have developed a Top Ten List for Starting a Successful Company (see page 44). Photocopy the list and consult it whenever you need some advice or inspiration. To create a Top Ten List of your own, write down what you've learned about starting a business, then number each idea. Keep your list handy in your wallet, locker, or place of business. Survey successful entrepreneurs in your area to get more ideas for your list.

7. Create a speakers' bureau for entrepreneurs in your school or community. You can call your chamber of commerce and/or local business groups to find possible speakers who could make presentations at your community center or school. Develop a form that includes each speaker's name, address, phone number, FAX number, topic, and time of availability. Make a directory of the resources and speakers to give to other entrepreneurs that you know. The speakers could make their presentations individually or through a panel discussion.

8. Start a fund for students in your school who need a small business loan. Ask for contributions from local businesses and find a bank that will hold your deposited funds. To get people interested in contributing money to the fund, hold a competition for the best business plan. Offer the loan to the person with the winning entry.

9. Think environmentally: What product could you make and sell using old tires, beverage cans, glass products, newspapers, or plastic containers? Many people prefer to buy products made from recycled materials to help save the earth. Ask your friends and family members to help you collect the items you plan to use. When you market your product, be sure to note that it was made from recycled materials.

10. Create and celebrate Girls and Young Women Entrepreneurs Week. Have local female business owners help with ideas for presentations and with scheduling, locations, etc. You may want to develop this idea locally, statewide, nationally, or internationally. You never know how far a good idea will go!

11. What are the start-up costs for your business? Do you have to invest in any equipment or supplies? If so, can you get people to donate the items instead? If you'll be paying for the supplies yourself, be sure to shop around to get the best possible price.

12. Some products, like Elizabeth Low's Happy Hand, just make life more fun. What product could you develop to help relieve stress and tension? What product might help people to laugh or to just enjoy life?

Service Businesses

Emily Bergson-Shilcock

The Destination of Independence

At eighteen years of age, Emily Bergson-Shilcock is entering school for the first time. That's because Emily was home schooled all of her life, along with her two sisters, Amanda and Julia, and her brother, Nicholas. Home schooling allowed Emily to go out into the world to learn through real-life experiences. She was accepted to Beaver College in Pennsylvania without submitting any grades or SAT scores. Emily was raised by her parents—Susan, a teacher, and Peter, an educational consultant—in a converted barn outside of Philadelphia. While growing up, she enjoyed volunteering at a home for disabled children, tutoring children in need, inventing, taking and teaching classical ballet, studying violin, and sharing her music with senior citizens. Just after her seventeenth birthday, she opened her own store, the Destination of Independence, selling products to make life easier for the elderly and for people with disabilities.

ON A COOL SPRING DAY, THE DOOR TO MY STORE OPENED AND IN walked one of my first customers. As she looked around at my products, her eyes settled on the self-opening scissors. She looked over at me and said, "I have really weak hands. How do these work?"

While walking over to show her, I replied, "Please pick them up, slide the safety latch off, and try them out on this fabric. They're self-opening, so they'll spring back open each time, and most people find them much easier on their hand muscles."

Emily Bergson-Shilcock

"How clever!" she said, as she cut the fabric easily. "I've never seen anything like these before."

She proceeded to test several more items and was especially delighted with the plug puller and the capscrew jar opener. She said, "I live alone and am often frustrated when I can't get a jar open. It's so clever that you have sample products so I can try things out before I buy them."

After making her selections, she placed several products on my sales desk, and I began to write her receipt and to ring up the products on the cash register. It was so thrilling to be dealing with a real customer! As I pushed the amount-tendered button on the cash register, the drawer opened and I remembered the thousands of

Emily in front of her store

times I'd played store as a child with the real electronic cash register I'd received at the age of ten. My dream of owning a store had come true after years of pretending.

I was home schooled all of my life. My parents wanted to provide me with lots of opportunities to learn through real work and through access to the world. Starting at the age of three, I loved counting money and playing store. At the age of seven, I opened my own checking account and learned how to balance my checkbook.

Throughout my childhood, I started many small businesses, such as running a bakery, selling blank books, organizing children's garage sales, selling books for my parents at educational conferences, and founding and directing summer camps. At the age of twelve, I began volunteering at a local clothing store and soon became a paid employee.

I had many volunteer experiences that helped me to gain leadership and business skills. I did volunteer work for an environmental group, tutored underprivileged children, helped out at a home for children with disabilities, and gave tours at a historical home. All of these undertakings helped me to gain confidence in dealing with people and taught me to appreciate the value of helping others.

For six years, I was also part of a community service violin quintet with my two sisters and two friends. We played at over 160 nursing homes and retirement homes, senior centers, and even at the White House. I became more sensitive to the challenges and needs of the elderly and disabled. In addition, my mother got rheumatoid arthritis, and I became aware of the daily challenges she faced. My love for business and my sensitivity to and awareness of those with physical restrictions came together and inspired me to create the Destination of Independence, a retail store selling products to make daily living easier for senior citizens and people with disabilities.

I put my ideas into action when I found a retail location with reasonable rent. My sights were set on a small store located right on the main road through town. I met with a lawyer, and I read books and researched setting up a business in Pennsylvania. From my reading I learned about sales tax* and licenses. I set up utility accounts to pay for gas, electricity, and water, and I opened a business bank account.

Even though I was only seventeen, I was treated respectfully and in a businesslike manner until I reached the bank. At the bank, I was told that I wasn't allowed to open a business account unless I had someone over the age of eighteen as the primary signer. Not only was I offended, but I also felt discriminated against. I'd had a personal checking account starting at the age of seven and a savings account since age twelve to save up for the car I bought myself at sixteen. However, I held my tongue and asked my older sister to be the primary signer. My feeling is that everyone started small and grew because someone decided to take a risk on them. Many small businesses have gone on to become successful nationally, and I hope mine will, too.

My next step was to obtain the initial inventory for my store. I researched products through catalogs, in the *Thomas Register* (a set of resource volumes on businesses, often found in libraries),

---

*To learn more about sales tax, see p. 145.

and by interviewing people who have rheumatoid arthritis, carpal tunnel syndrome, multiple sclerosis, etc. I applied for open accounts as a wholesaler (when you buy goods as a wholesaler, you purchase them in high quantity at a lower price to resell). I also did lots and lots of paperwork, phoning, and faxing.

My start-up budget of four thousand dollars (one thousand of my own and a loan of three thousand from my parents) covered everything I needed. I was able to rent my store, design and install slatwall and display fixtures, purchase start-up inventory, mail out grand-opening invitations, and pay for the required business licenses and deposits on utility accounts. I also made the decision to be open only three days a week so I could keep a healthy balance of activities in my life.

My family was very supportive in helping me translate my dream into a reality. Initial help came from my parents, although my goal was to do as much as possible on my own. My father helped me with some of the store construction and with the making of model displays for several products. My mother helped me to create some of the initial brochures and press releases, to write descriptive signs for every product, and to try out products to see which ones worked best. My sisters and my brother have helped with stocking the merchandise, sending out mailings, and filling orders.

My vision was to provide a homey and friendly atmosphere where my customers could relax, even sit while they shop, and test out sample products to see how they work for them. I provided a mini gardening center to try the tools in the dirt, a kitchen counter equipped with jars for opening and with carrots for peeling, a lamp with a big lamp switch, and doorknobs with extensions and easy grips—all easily accessible for people to try.

I'm always learning from my customers. After all, they're the ones who have to face daily challenges, and when they tell me about products they wish existed, I get inspired to figure out ways to make such products. For example, several customers shared with me their trouble carrying personal items while trying to maneuver their walkers. Some already had walker bags but found that the pockets were too small. As a result, I designed an improved walker bag with larger pockets that I now sell at less than half the cost of other commercial versions.

Because of my unique experiences with people who face such challenges, the *uncommon* customer has become my *common* one. A customer who stands out in my mind is an elderly woman who's legally blind. She walked through my door with her hands outstretched and said in a soft voice, "Can you help me? Do you have a lighted magnifier?" She proceeded to tell me that even though she was legally blind, she'd walked alone from her apartment building several blocks away. I was astounded that someone who's blind could go anywhere without another person or a seeing-eye dog. I unwrapped the magnifier, installed the batteries, and took her hands and showed her how to operate it. The look on her face as she said "I will now be able to read the headlines in the newspaper" was so satisfying.

I remember thinking how courageous she was to have come so far alone. She told me that she had no family and lived by herself. As I counted out her change, I helped to sort it into the different pockets

Emily with a customer

she had for every coin. I don't think I could ever forget the smile on her face as she walked cautiously out the door and thanked me for helping her. She has become a regular customer.

My business has evolved tremendously since its opening in April of 1995. I've expanded it in many ways. I now give free demonstrations to retirement homes, senior centers, support groups, etc., where I bring a selection of products for participants to try, and I speak about specific features and how they can help in daily living. I also supply several of the local retirement homes with a selection of my products to offer in their gift shops. Both of these aspects of my business have helped to make more people aware of the Destination of Independence.

In addition, I've been featured in many local newspapers and I've appeared in short human-interest stories for the TV news. This publicity has brought new customers to my store. Truthfully, I like the publicity—I like to open up the newspaper and see my picture or watch the news and hear about myself. This kind of recognition can be one of the rewards that comes only after hard work.

Because I've been so exhilarated and motivated by managing my business, my learning has flourished. I've become proficient in many areas including using computers, speaking in public, managing finances, writing ads, asserting myself under pressure, learning how to do research and to contact wholesalers, and tailoring lectures and demonstrations to specific audiences.

I have many plans for the expansion of the Destination of Independence that I'm keeping on hold until I finish my education at Beaver College. I'll intentionally be keeping my business small until graduation, and I'll also be creating and refining plans for the future. In the coming years at school, I plan to study other prosperous entrepreneurs, to learn from their successes and mistakes, and to discover how to create new marketing strategies. I would also like to develop new product ideas and try my hand at more inventing.

I hope that in the future people will hear the name the Destination of Independence, or even Emily, and know what my store carries and who I am. Many people laugh now and think that I can't do it, but I know that people can do anything if they set their minds to it. I can imagine having large stores that are user-friendly and customer service-oriented.

When people discover that I started my business at the age of seventeen, they often ask what advice I have for other young entrepreneurs. Although people will create their own "right way," I would offer these guidelines:

- Have a vision.

- Stay on target.

- Make sure you're doing something you love because you'll be spending lots of time doing it.

- Be comfortable adapting and refining your work until it really suits you.

- See the value of nurturing a small idea, knowing that a strong foundation will help to grow a big idea.

- See the value of volunteering to gain free insight and experience while helping others.

- Document all of your work—always take pictures and save any printed material to help you with further advertising.

- And remember the old saying: Success breeds success.

Owning and operating a business of my own has given me the chance to be self-directed and to control my own destiny. I have the power to reach for any goal and to achieve it. I don't need to wait for someone to tell me what to do, and I don't need to *wish* I could put a plan of mine into action; I can just do it. It's a magnificent feeling.

Mary Elizabeth Anne Curtice

Little Mary's Ray of Sunshine

Mary Elizabeth Anne Curtice is fifteen and lives with her parents, Peter and Claire, who are both high school teachers; her seven-year-old sister, Susan; and her sixteen-year-old brother, Raymond. The Curtice family's home is in Leander, Texas.

Mary's interests include fencing, drama, science, Odyssey of the Mind, student council, and her church youth group. She hopes to one day continue her schooling at Stanford, Notre Dame University, or DePaul University, where she plans to major in pre-law with a psychology minor. Once out of school, she'd like to continue her flower business and become an attorney and a judge.

WHEN I WAS ELEVEN, I STARTED FENCING. I LIKED IT AND THE COACH said I was really good. The coach began to talk about taking a group of fencers to the Junior Olympics. That sounded like fun, and I wanted to go. The problem was that the trip would be expensive.

When I asked my parents if they would allow me to go, they said they were unable to give me the financial support I needed to compete in fencing at the national level. I decided to try to start my own business so I could earn the money for fencing. After talking to my mom and dad about possible businesses and fundraisers, I felt that there might be an opportunity for a flower delivery business during the summer when school was out.

**Mary Elizabeth
Anne Curtice**

I started my business in Georgetown, Texas, which is the county seat. (A few years later, my family moved to Leander, Texas.) There are many government offices and attorneys in Georgetown. Because the downtown area was only three blocks from my house, I knew that I could walk to find customers and to deliver my flowers.

To start my business, I went to the local grocery store and found that I could buy flowers at a discount if I bought enough. I was going to buy the vases there, but the price was too high. I realized that if I paid too much for my materials, I would have to charge a higher price to my customers, which I didn't want to do. I looked around and discovered that if I bought the vases at local thrift shops, they were only ten cents each. I borrowed one hundred dollars from my parents so I could stock up on the supplies I needed for my business.

I then began to practice my sales pitch. My parents listened to it time and time again, giving me suggestions and helping me to get it right. I decided to name my business Little Mary's Sunshine. With my sales pitch ready and with flyers I had designed on our family computer, I set off. I spent several days walking around the square in Georgetown carrying a Polaroid picture of a sample vase of flowers. I had learned to arrange the flowers with help from my grandma, who has taken floral arrangement classes.

When customers wanted my flowers, I took a five dollar deposit and found out where in the downtown area they wanted me to deliver them. On Monday mornings, I took a vase of flowers to my customers or anyone to whom they wanted flowers sent. Each following Monday, I took fresh flowers to replace the old ones I had delivered the previous week. Most of the time, the old flowers were still alive and fresh looking, so I rearranged them and delivered them to local nursing homes. After the fourth week, I asked my customers if they wanted to continue with flower deliveries for the next month.

It didn't take long for me to get thirty customers. Although this number may not sound very large, I was able to make about six dollars profit from each customer each month, and most of the customers signed up for a whole summer of flower deliveries.

The first summer that I was in business, I was able to pay for all of my supplies, return the money I'd borrowed from my parents, and make a profit of about four hundred dollars. The check for one hundred dollars that I wrote to my mom and dad was the first check I'd ever written for such a large amount of money.

The next summer, I got an early start on my business. Because I now had experience and a list of clients from the year before, I was able to expand to forty-five customers. People soon approached me and asked, "Are you the flower girl?" They would give me a five dollar deposit on the spot and request that I deliver flowers to their workplace. Word-of-mouth was and still is the way most of my customers hear of

Mary and her brother, Raymond, choosing flowers for a Monday delivery

my services. People still refer to me as "the flower girl" or "Little Mary," even though I'm older now.

During the second year of business, the flower prices at the local grocery store had increased dramatically. I began thinking of getting a wholesale license so I could buy flowers in bulk at a lower price. The problem was the ninety dollar fee. I wrote to Rick Perry, the agricultural commissioner, told him about my business, and explained that the fee was outrageous for me. He personally wrote back to me, and a wholesale license was included with the note! Since then, I've been buying my flowers wholesale.

One of the problems that I faced with my business was not realizing how much thirty vases of flowers could weigh. I would put the vases into a wagon and pull the wagon downtown, but I couldn't pull it up the hill between my house and the local square. At about that time, my brother, Raymond, was begging me for a job. So I hired him to pull the wagon and to help deliver the flowers. We argued a lot about how much I should pay him. Finally, we decided that he should get 15 percent of the gross profits and that the business should pay for a drink and snack at the end of each delivery run. Because we live in Texas, where the summers can get pretty hot, we look forward to a cold drink and ice cream after all of the deliveries have been made.

During the second year of my business, my brother became a partner. With the increase in customers, it had become impossible for me to do without an employee, and Raymond threatened to quit if I didn't make him a partner. Now he does all of the paperwork on our computer, arranges some of the vases, and pulls our new carrier, which attaches to a bike (this allows us to cart more flowers than the wagon did). We changed the name of the business to Little Mary's Ray of Sunshine to include Raymond's name.

My advice to young women who are just starting a business is to allow people to open doors for you. My parents have been a great help in getting my business off the ground and in arranging and delivering the flowers. My first customers helped me by encouraging me and believing in me. One of my customers paid for my first business cards and even contacted the local newspaper, which ran several stories about my business. Another customer allowed me to trade flowers for our post-delivery snacks.

Because of my business, I've met judges, lawyers, librarians, government officials, businesspeople, and even an author. I've acquired several diverse skills including bookkeeping, public speaking, and marketing know-how. I've also learned how to dress and to present myself so that I'm taken seriously as a businesswoman. Perhaps the most important lesson I've learned is that the customer is always right.

My business has really grown, and we've expanded from Georgetown, to Round Rock, and into downtown Austin, now that Raymond can drive. We currently deliver the flowers from the car instead of using a wagon or a bike. This summer will mark my fifth year in business, and I hope to be the next Bill Gates (the founder of Microsoft and a multimillionaire!).

Melissa Poe

Kids For A
Clean Environment
(Kids F.A.C.E.)*

Melissa Poe is an eighteen-year-old from Nashville, Tennessee. She lives there with her dad, Pat, who owns an industrial hardware company, and her mom, Trish, who is Executive Director of Kids For A Clean Environment. Melissa has an older brother named Mason. Melissa has always been very persistent, determined, and resourceful—characteristics that led her, at age nine, to start a campaign to encourage people to protect the environment. In 1989, Melissa founded an environmental club that she eventually helped grow into an organization that has over 300,000 members. Melissa enjoys spending time with friends, participating in cross-country track, swimming, and seeing movies.

W HEN YOU'RE NINE YEARS OLD AND THINKING OF WHAT YOUR FUTURE will be, you don't imagine the world to be a place where you can't survive—with no trees or flowers, clean water to drink, or fresh air to breathe. I didn't either, until I saw a TV program that showed this "what if" world that could become a reality if people didn't take steps to protect our natural resources. The message of the show, however, was that it's not too late and that people who care can do something. That's when I decided I wanted to be someone who cared—someone who *did* something. I figured that since our pollution problem was so

---

*If you're interested in learning more about the Kids F.A.C.E. organization, write to: Kids F.A.C.E., P.O. Box 158254, Nashville, TN 37215.

Melissa Poe

big, I'd need a lot of people to help solve it. So I began my campaign to get people involved.

My idea was to mobilize people who care. I began an ongoing campaign to encourage kids and adults to get involved in their communities and to solve environmental problems. I started a club for kids called Kids For A Clean Environment, or Kids F.A.C.E., in Nashville. My environmental club for young people eventually became an international organization.

To get things started, I wrote some letters, and the first one was to George Bush, who was president at the time. I figured that if *he* got involved, he could influence a lot of people—after all, he could get on TV any time he wanted. I also figured that because he was the president, people would listen when he talked.

It took the president twelve weeks to write to me. Actually, he never did write to me—all I received from his office was a form letter telling me to stay in school and not to do drugs. Fortunately, during those twelve weeks I didn't just sit around and wait for a reply to my letter. I wrote letters to other political leaders such as my state's senators, members of Congress, and mayor. I wrote articles for the newspaper and did a news commentary on the local TV station.

I also called existing environmental organizations, such as the Sierra Club and Greenpeace, and asked them what I could do to help protect our natural resources. With each call, I was informed that there was nothing I could do because I was too young. I became really frustrated by this answer, which is why I founded an environmental club just for kids. It started with six members at my elementary school. The club was underwritten by Wal-Mart, and membership was free.

Starting an organization is one thing; helping it to grow is another. This ongoing effort demanded many volunteer hours and

Melissa at an award ceremony

Members of Kids F.A.C.E. celebrating Earth Day 1995

on-the-job training averaging twelve to fifteen hours per week. My outreach activities required me to write and deliver speeches before a variety of groups—from an inner-city development in Mobile, Alabama, to members of the Earth Summit in Brazil. The media presented many stories about my efforts, which resulted in lots of correspondence from youth around the world. I answered every letter.

Because I wanted all of the members of my growing organization to be able to stay in touch with one another, I developed an organization-wide newsletter. I also established the "home" chapter of the club, where we could create and carry out pilot projects and successfully develop them into international efforts. Through all of this, I've been fortunate to have the support of my family, teachers, mentors, and counselors, as well as local businesses and community leaders. These leaders, plus some of my friends, volunteer to serve on the governing board to help guide the activities of Kids F.A.C.E.

Although I had the support of many caring people, others ignored my attempts to start and run my own organization, while still others laughed and taunted me for my efforts. The major obstacle I faced was the perception many people held about youth. I constantly heard, "You can't do that. You're just a kid!" Persistence is what helped me. I found that if you keep going and continue to encourage others to get involved, you'll find people who care.

Over the past eight years, the most noticeable result of my work has been the growth of Kids F.A.C.E. Boys and girls in all fifty states and twenty foreign countries, regardless of age, race, or economic status, have benefited from this effort. Many kids have written to me, asking what they can do to help and sharing their frustration of not knowing what to do. I let them know by my example that they, too, can get involved in saving the earth.

In addition to starting school recycling programs, cleaning up litter along highways, and planting trees, my organization has worked to create the Kids Earth Flag, a visual expression of how young people see the world. It was unveiled in 1995 in Washington, D.C. The flag consists of 20,000 fabric squares, created by individual kids and stitched together by volunteers. The flag has toured schools and communities across the nation and continues to grow as kids send in more squares.

When I began this effort, I wanted to reach people and encourage them to care about their world. I believe that when people care enough, they'll get involved. I feel that I'm accomplishing my goals in Kids F.A.C.E., and that the organization I started will continue to exist as long as there are kids who care.

Looking back, I've learned that if you want to motivate others to get involved, you must start with yourself. Develop your skills of motivation, leadership, communication, and entrepreneurship. Once you've done that, you become an example for others to follow.

If you see a problem in the world, find a way to fix it. You can do this by starting an organization, as I did; by volunteering your time and energy; or by any other means you can find. Get involved—even just do a simple thing like writing a letter. The ultimate responsibility always lies within you, and opportunities are the ones you create.

Theresa and Beth Baily

Pet-Sitting Club (PSC)

Theresa and Beth Baily are sisters who attend the same elementary school near Detroit, Michigan. Theresa is ten and Beth is nine. Their mother, Joan, is Assistant Director of their local YMCA, and their father, Tim, is a technician at the Ford Motor Company.

Both girls are on the school swim team (the Blue Racers) and are members of the same Girl Scout troop. They are also in business together. Although they spend a great deal of time with each other, the sisters have diverse interests. Theresa is involved in student council and the school's radio club. Beth enjoys doing art, creating stories, and singing.

We STARTED OUR BUSINESS AFTER READING A *BABYSITTERS CLUB* story about Karen's kitty cat club. In the story, the characters lost their pet-sitting job because they were too young. We got the idea to start a club of our own. We thought it would be fun to work with other girls and to feel like we belonged to something.

At first, we tried a mystery-solving club, but there weren't any mysteries to solve! Next, we tried starting a pet-sitting club with some friends. This wasn't too successful because some people in the club didn't have enough pets in their neighborhood. One girl had a job lined up to pet-sit a lizard, but it ran away before she started the job! We decided to forget about having a pet-sitting club with friends.

Beth *(left)* **and Theresa Baily**

These setbacks didn't stop us, though. We now have our own pet-sitting business called Pet-Sitting Club, or PSC. Our customers are people in our neighborhood. Many of them work long hours and go away on a lot of business trips. We take care of their pets when they're gone. Running this business is great fun because we love animals. Most of the pet owners in our area now rely on us instead of the kennel.

Starting a business was more of a challenge than we thought it would be. Pet-sitting isn't just feeding and walking the animals, then going home. We spend our after-school time playing with the animals so they get their exercise and don't get lonely. Plus we have to take care of the animals before school and still get to school on time. We've really learned to use our time wisely.

We've also discovered that pets have personalities and special needs. For example, we pet-sit a pug dog who really loves kids. To keep him happy, we take him with us when we go to the swimming pool during the summer so he can be around a lot of children. Other

Theresa *(left)* and Beth walking their favorite pug

kids give him attention when we go in the pool. We've also taken care of elderly animals. One of the old cats that we cared for had to have its food ground up so it was easier to chew and swallow. Many of the pets we take care of come to our home for much of the day so they can have constant attention. They've really become a part of our family!

Because of our business, we've gotten to know the people in our neighborhood. We feel more of a sense of community. We plan to keep our business in the neighborhood, instead of expanding, because it's easy for us to walk to our clients' houses. We have lots of customers here, too.

We continue to attract new business mainly by word-of-mouth. That's the best advertising of all. We feel good knowing that our clients trust us enough to recommend us to others. As owners of a pet-sitting business, we have to be responsible enough to go into people's homes, feed their pets the right amount of food, know who to call if there's an emergency situation with a pet, and remember to lock the doors as we leave. People depend on us to do a good job.

We're experimenting with creating business flyers to find more customers in our neighborhood. By using a special computer program, we're learning to make a flyer on our home computer. The flyer, which we plan to leave in people's doorways around the community, describes our business and our rates. Our goal is to eventually pet-sit every animal in our neighboorhood.

Our mom has been a huge support along the way. She puts up with the fact that we bring our clients' pets home with us for visits. More importantly, she helps us to stay organized and to follow through. We've learned that while it's fun to jump in and start a business, you have to follow through with what you start. If you avoid the duties and responsibilities of your business, your clients

The Baily sisters take care of many different kinds of dogs as part of their pet-sitting service.

will suffer and they won't want to do business with you again. It's very important to live up to your customers' expectations.

The key to our success has been providing a service that people really need. We're also very affordable—we only charge three dollars per day for dogs and cats. We go out of our way to provide little extras for each client, which is good customer service. We listen to what our customers need, and we make sure we understand everything they want us to do. Running a business has taught us to be responsible and committed.

If you're thinking of starting your own business, you might consider doing so with a partner. You could find a family member or friend who might like to join you. Make sure this person is someone you get along with, like, and trust. In a partnership, trust is very important. You need to feel confident that the other person will give 100 percent and will do her best in every aspect of the business.

Keep trying and don't give up if you experience any setbacks. We learned about being flexible when something doesn't work. Instead of getting upset about it, find what *does* work. It will be worth it because owning a business truly has many rewards.

Mandy Baar

Martha's Sweet Shop

Twenty-three-year-old Mandy Baar grew up in Grand Rapids, Michigan, with her parents, Jim, a foreman, and Jan, a marketing specialist. Mandy has two sisters, Lori and Cara, who are both in college.

Mandy graduated from Grand Rapids Christian High School in June of 1991. She then spent two years at Calvin College in Grand Rapids and two years at Grand Valley State University in Allendale, Michigan. She's studying elementary education but has also taken business classes. Mandy spends seven months each year on Mackinac Island, located in the straits of Michigan. She got involved in Junior Achievement in her junior year of high school and continues to be active in teaching the elementary and middle school programs both on Mackinac Island and in Grand Rapids. Mandy is the youngest person ever to sit on the Junior Achievement Board of Directors for Northern Michigan.

IN JANUARY OF 1994, I WAS A SOPHOMORE IN COLLEGE, AND I BEGAN TO think about where to work for the summer. I decided to go away and enjoy a new area because I love to travel. I applied for jobs at different businesses and parks around the state and country. I was accepted at a bakery/ice cream shop—Martha's Sweet Shop—on Mackinac Island in the straits of Michigan, a place I had visited when I won a trip through Junior Achievement.

I loved working at Martha's Sweet Shop as the baker and housemother that summer. I was employed there the following summer, too, and found out that the shop was for sale. Because I'd worked for the owner (Martha), several people suggested that I buy the shop. It became quite a joke for me because I was a college student struggling

Mandy Baar

to keep up with my tuition and rent costs. How could I ever afford an expensive business on Mackinac Island?

When a friend of my mom's showed interest in investing in the business, I began to think it might be possible to purchase the shop. I worked on a business plan that I could present to other possible investors. But by the end of the summer season, I still hadn't bought the shop, and I had to return to school. Fortunately, it was still for sale during the fall.

Over that winter, Martha and I talked about the possibility of my buying the shop the next season. I took business classes at school, and the following summer I worked for Martha as the shop manager and baker in preparation for purchasing the shop in the fall. We worked out a deal: If I could give Martha a quarter of the total cost as a down payment on the shop, the rest could be on a land contract. This means that I pay Martha a fixed amount of money each year until my debt is paid off. If I don't pay, she can take over the shop again.

I had to come up with the down payment, so I decided to talk to my family about a loan instead of going to a bank. I wrote up my business plan, then approached members of my immediate and extended family. I told them I would return the money, with interest, over the next few years. My family was very supportive, and soon I had the amount needed to pay Martha. The shop became mine! We signed all of the papers on October 23, 1995, making Martha's Sweet Shop officially mine as a sole proprietorship.*

I spent that winter preparing to open the shop for my first season as owner. There was a lot of work to do, including hiring the employees, purchasing all of the necessary supplies, and filling out all of the paperwork for the government and for bookkeeping. I worked two full-time jobs during that time to save money for supplies, rent, utilities, and payroll.

The first summer was very difficult and stressful, but rewarding for me. I worked about twelve to sixteen hours a day, seven days a week. I began baking at 4:30 A.M. each morning, and the shop stayed open until 10:00 P.M.

I had seven full-time and three part-time employees, most of whom were college students. Each day, I was busy managing my employees; anticipating any problems; doing the ordering, baking, and cleaning; thinking of new ideas to try in the shop; counting the money; keeping track of the accounting; paying the bills; and much more. Through all of this, the shop had a very successful season financially. Because I didn't take a paycheck from the money my business earned, I was even able to pay back some of my family members who had loaned money to me.

At the shop, we try out new ideas each year, which has helped the business to improve. Last summer, we added cappuccino, bagels, and new muffin recipes. Next summer, we're hoping to add a few more muffins, some new frozen yogurt flavors, and more sundaes, in addition to supplying more of the island's bed-and-

*To learn more about sole proprietorships, see pp. 144–145.

Mandy standing in front of her shop

breakfasts with cinnamon rolls, muffins, and bagels delivered fresh from the oven daily.

I'll also be remodeling before reopening in the spring, to give the shop a fresh, new look. Right now, the shop's walls are covered with mirrors and an ornate border. I'm going to put up more of a floral border, repaint the walls, and install a new floor. All of this should make the shop more inviting and reflect a coffee shop and ice-cream parlor look. I think the regular customers on the island will appreciate these updates, since the shop has looked the same for nine years. Plus I'll feel a stronger sense of ownership when the shop reflects my own decorating style. I think it's important for shop owners to continue to change things, not only for the customers but also for themselves. This keeps the business new and exciting. With these ideas and other ones I'm working on, I hope my shop will grow bigger.

My business is unique because it's only open for six months of the year. But those six months are very intense, since many tourists visit the island for its beauty, history, and unique atmosphere. These tourists crowd my shop during the summer season.

Owning my own business is extremely rewarding for me. I'm very happy to say that my shop is where I love to be, and I enjoy going to work each day.

If you're thinking of becoming an entrepreneur, my best piece of advice is to make sure you really understand what your business will involve. I've found that many people think that owning a business means you don't have to do any work. When I teach Junior Achievement in the schools, students often remark how great it must be to own a shop because I "don't have to do any work and can spend the day telling other people what to do." In response, I always describe my typical day to them, and I explain that maybe someday I'll be able to work fewer hours but for now I need to be in the shop all the time to run things and to supervise.

Mandy showing off her freshly baked cinnamon rolls

Another piece of advice: Get some experience working in your field of interest. That's what I did. Working at the shop before I bought it helped me to be sure that I really wanted to own it. You need to know that the business you're choosing is one that you'll enjoy, because you don't want to get stuck working sixteen hours a day in a place that you absolutely can't stand. Also, you need to have a good understanding of managing money and paperwork.

When you start thinking of how to get the money that you'll need to start your business, don't eliminate the possibility of borrowing from your family. (For some people, borrowing money from family members may cause problems, so don't be afraid to go to a bank.) The family members who loaned money to me have shown a lot of interest in my shop, and they visit me and help out when I need assistance. I feel that I can ask them for advice when I'm struggling with a problem. As a single young woman, I've found this to be a good support system.

Katy and Allie Rosenbaum

The Magic of Katy and Allie Rose

Katy and Allie Rosenbaum are sisters from Cary, North Carolina. They have a unique business—their own magic act. Their family is made up of their dad, Fred, an electrical engineer, and their mom, Dorothy, a homemaker. They also have an umbrella cockatoo named Gracie.

Katy is thirteen and in eighth grade. She enjoys reading, swimming, travel, music, art, and, of course, magic. She's a member of the All-A honor roll (three years straight), the National Junior Honor Society, the Society of Young Magicians, and the International Brotherhood of Magicians (IBM), and she plays first chair French horn in the symphonic band at school. Katy has performed in many plays and has won awards in music and academics. Her sister, Allie, is ten and enjoys magic, swimming, dance, and basketball. Allie's favorite subject in school is language arts. She won a second and third place award in the statewide Rising Star Literary Contest for Poetry; she also earned second place in a statewide writing contest.

K**ATY**: HOW DOES A PAIR OF YOUNG SISTERS BECOME ENTREPRENEURS in magic? It all started when I was only two. Our family was on an airplane, and a man was making balloon animals. I was enchanted when the man handed me a balloon in the shape of a dog. After that, my dad went to a local magic shop to learn how to make balloon animals and rekindled his childhood interest in magic.

Our family eventually started attending conventions and purchasing magic supplies. In 1989, we attended an International

Katy Rosenbaum

Brotherhood of Magicians convention in California, where vendors were selling magic supplies. I wanted a magic trick that cost eighteen dollars, but my dad said it was too expensive. Gallagher, a well-known comedian, was standing nearby and overheard our conversation. He looked down at me, smiled, and said, "Hey, I'll buy it for you." With this as a start, my magic was on its way.

In 1992, we went to a magic shop that had a miniature zig-zag illusion. In the zig-zag illusion, you put your assistant in a box, "cut" the assistant into thirds, and pull out the middle box. This box happened to be just the right size to fit my sister, Allie. The Magic of Katy and Allie Rose was born!

That summer, we attended an International Brotherhood of Magicians convention in Salt Lake City, Utah. We had been practicing our magic tricks and took our act on the road with us. We performed at a private party and at the local Shriners Hospital as an act of community service for the organization. At about that time, Austin, Texas, became our new home. Austin has a wonderful magic community—locally, there's an IBM Ring, a Society of American Magicians (SAM) assembly, and a summer magic day camp.

As our interest in magic and performing grew, we decided to compete in a regional convention called the Texas Association of Magicians (TAOM), which meets every Labor Day weekend. We polished our act and went to the TAOM meeting in 1992. Although we didn't win, we put on a good show! During the following year, we performed on a volunteer basis at local schools, churches, and malls. We were slowly becoming known as "The Girl Magicians from Austin."

In 1993, we were hired to perform at the TAOM convention in front of 2,000 spectators. This event really changed our career. We received media attention, resulting in other bookings. Soon we were performing at the local children's museum, working fairs and other venues, and assisting other magicians with their shows. We earned from twenty-five to fifty dollars per show, but we continued our volunteer performances, too.

At home, we kept practicing and changing our act. We added music, props, and special effects. When our local library asked us

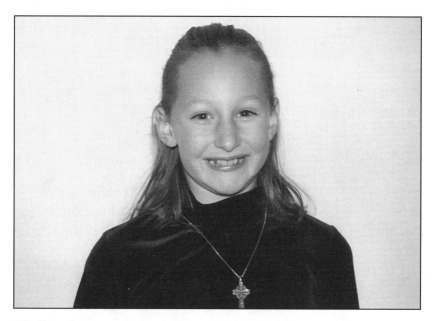

Allie Rosenbaum

to help promote the summer reading program, a new opportunity arose for us. One of the children at the program enjoyed our act enough to ask us to perform at her upcoming birthday party. We refused at first because we didn't think we were old enough to be responsible for managing a party full of children. The family kept asking, though, and we finally agreed. We developed a birthday party show that features about thirty minutes of magic, plus balloon animals. The cost started at fifty dollars per show and is now seventy-five dollars.

In the summer of 1994, I went to California to attend a weeklong magic camp called West Coast Wizards. Allie joined me at West Coast Wizards in 1995 and 1996. The camp improved our techniques and offered us the chance to meet other young people interested in magic and to be instructed by famous magicians. During the

Katy *(left)* **and Allie making balloon sculptures**

rest of the year, we continued attending conventions and lectures to try to learn all we could about the art of magic.

Allie has progressed from an assistant to a partner in the act, and our stage performances have improved. In 1995, we developed a western-themed stage act called "Hello Texas" for the TAOM convention, and the act won first place. We were asked to present this act in Las Vegas for the Society of American Magicians convention in the summer of 1996. Our magic continues to change, and we never know where we might go!

Today, our business mainly consists of several stage acts, a birthday party show, and balloon sculpturing. We enjoy running the business and improving our act. One of our best marketing strategies is performing on a volunteer basis so we can get name recognition and attention from the press. In addition, we've worked with a public relations specialist who designed a logo for us. We've also created press releases and a brochure about our business, and we're on the Internet. Word-of-mouth is our greatest promotion—kids see us and tell their parents that they want us to perform at their birthday parties.

Our business has helped to develop our confidence and stage presence, and to bring our family closer together. Performing together as sisters has made us partners and close friends. The money we've earned has helped us to invest in more magic supplies, to improve our act, and to pay for publicity. We also use our earnings to help support a needy child in Peru, a commitment we made when we first started working.

Our business has enabled us to meet many magicians, famous and not-so-famous, and to make many friends. We're grateful for our parents' support and for the skills we've learned at the West Coast Wizards camp. Our local magic organization has always been there for us, offering feedback and ideas, and becoming our "extended family." The world of magic is mainly male- and adult-dominated. We're a unique act, and the encouragement we've received has helped us to go far.

My advice to other entrepreneurs is to work hard, have fun, take risks, and look for possibilities in the unexpected. Give of your time, talents, and money—it opens doors.

I don't know what the future holds for us. We may become famous magicians someday, or maybe magic will just be a hobby. So far, our magic business has offered us excitement, rewards, friends, and a good feeling for the help we give to others. What more could we want?

A<small>LLIE</small>: I<small>T'S HARD TO BELIEVE THAT ONLY A FEW YEARS AFTER SEEING</small> my first magic show, I'm now a professional magician. I started out as my sister's assistant in her magic show, and now we're full partners. We have our own business that has taken us from coast to coast, performing magic.

Having a business is fun and enjoyable. The business builds my self-esteem and has made me feel more comfortable in front of groups of strangers and friends. It's great to be making money while doing something I love to do.

During performances, I try to get to know the people in the audience and to make new friends. I love knowing that people enjoy our act. I work on my magic skills all of the time so that I can get even better. I practice magic tricks, juggling, and balloon sculpturing.

Running our magic business has been a very positive experience. But it's challenging, too. We have to rehearse our act a lot. Sometimes, I would rather be doing something else, but I know I have to practice if I want our performances to be good. Rehearsals can be frustrating, especially when we can't seem to get things right. But then it all comes together, and we start having fun again.

I have learned many things from running a business. First, if you don't promote your business, you won't have any customers. We work hard on promotion so we'll have lots of shows to do. Also, we have to invest more than just our time in the business—we also invest money that we earn. Magic props can be expensive. But it's definitely worth it!

If you want to start your own business, I have some advice. Be sure to advertise your business so people will know what you have to offer. You can use flyers, ads, or the Internet to advertise. Also, make sure that your business meets the needs of your customers. Talk to them to get their feedback. They may have good ideas about how you can improve what you do. Most of all, enjoy your business.

**The Rosenbaum
sisters in their
magic act**

I have found that being my sister's business partner has rewards. We support each other, and we help each other to become better performers. Even when we disagree about some aspects of our business, we know that we still love each other. We each give 100 percent to the business so we can go far.

I really recommend that any girl should have the courage to start her profession at a young age. Take it as far as you possibly can!

Barbara Campbell

Addition and
Subtraction Hair Firm

Barbara Campbell, age twenty-five, is the Chief Executive Officer (CEO) of Addition and Subtraction Hair Firm, a Manhattan-based salon that she founded at age twenty-three. Barbara has been starting businesses since she was sixteen and loves the challenges and excitement of being an entrepreneur.

In school, Barbara studied art, computers, and business marketing, and these classes taught her skills that have helped her with the salon. She spends her free time exercising, in-line skating, and doing other outdoor activities. Barbara has been featured in various articles in newspapers and in magazines, and she was interviewed on CNN's Sonya Live *and* Money Wheel. *She recently self-published a work-book called* Tools for Success: A Guide for Building Your Dreams.

*I*N ELEMENTARY SCHOOL, I WAS ALWAYS VERY CREATIVE, LOOKING FOR new and unusual ways of thinking and doing things. My real interest in becoming a businesswoman was sparked through my involvement with the National Foundation for Teaching Entrepreneurship (NFTE). My marketing teacher in high school, Mrs. Gutman, introduced me to the organization and motivated me to develop myself as a business leader. She's been a source of encouragement and strength for me; she taught me to believe in myself. Throughout high school, I took classes and did everything I could to learn about the world of business.

At age sixteen, I started my first business, Custom Designs and Handmade Bags. I worked hard to save money, to put my ideas

Barbara Campbell

together in a business plan, and to market my business. I also had fun designing and sewing bags of different types. This business satisfied the goals I had as a result of my marketing classes and participation in NFTE.

After graduating from high school, I attended the Fashion Institute of Technology and the Learning Institute of Beauty Science. During this time, I received a personal gift of money from my mother, and I put it together with the money I had already saved to create my second business, Addition and Subtraction Hair Firm.

My business has now been in existence for two years. The services include hair care, beauty care, and consultations. I'm also in the process of developing skin-care products and cosmetics. I'm making a profit and have already reached several goals for the business.

I would, however, still like to expand in several areas that would tie all of my interests—clothing, accessories, hair care, and skin care—together. My ultimate goal is to create a multidimensional, international corporation focusing on outer and inner beauty. I'm continuing my studies at college in the areas of business, marketing, and public relations.

I firmly believe that knowledge is power. Having an education is crucial to the success of your business and to your success in life. So don't ever stop learning! I also believe in dreams. Listen to the beat of

Barbara with some of her beauty products

your heart and follow the dream you desire. Live your dreams now and forever.

My marketing strategies include brochures and other types of printed ads, but word-of-mouth has been the most effective for me. I'm currently developing a newsletter as another type of service and as a marketing strategy. Plans are also underway for me to make more presentations and to hold more workshops across the country. I want to help inspire young women and men across the globe to learn to love themselves.

I've discovered that entrepreneurship has many benefits. I enjoy being in control of my own hours and being my own boss. I set my own goals and manage my time. If I'm having a difficult day with very few sales, I stay focused and find other ways to promote the business or any new ideas I may have. Entrepreneurship has also given me the opportunity to work with many interesting people. It makes me feel great to see the smiles on my clients' faces.

My advice to other girls and young women is to believe in yourself and to have faith. I believe that God can help you to learn to use your talents in a positive way. I also suggest that you find a network of friends and family to help give you moral support and love along the way. And don't forget to give back to those who've helped you get started. One of my goals is to give back to my mother, who sacrificed to help me.

I'm very proud of my accomplishments, but I have many more goals to achieve. I hope that God will bless my future and that my business will grow to reach international markets. I also hope to have a family of my own one day. I believe that an entrepreneur is a risk-taker and a visionary who's traveling the road to success. I'm making my own path down that road.

Megan Leaf

Love Box, Limited

Megan Leaf, age sixteen, was diagnosed at the age of three with neurofibromatosis, a genetic disorder causing tumors. Megan's tumor is on her optic nerve, resulting in blindness in her right eye and other complications. Because of the tumor, Megan is a frequent outpatient at Johns Hopkins Children's Center, which is near her home in Bel Air, Maryland.

Her father, Michael, is an attorney, and her mother, Deborah, is a kindergarten teacher. Megan's sister, Brigid, is seventeen and attends college. Megan's immediate and extended family have always been sources of support in her life, and she talks openly with them about her goals, school issues, and medical problems. She's been an active member of the student activities club, the forensics team, and the drama club at her school. In her spare time, Megan collects teddy bears, reads, and volunteers.

T HE OFFICIAL NAME OF MY COMPANY IS LOVE BOX, LIMITED, BUT IT'S more often referred to as Love Box. I started the business in 1991, then in 1993, I incorporated* as a nonprofit organization providing gift bags full of toys and activities to patients at the Johns Hopkins Children's Center. I personally decorate and fill each bag with a coloring book, crayons, a game, a stuffed animal, and a toy that matches the season or holiday. I deliver an average of thirty bags per month.

During any holiday season, I decorate the bags and fill them to reflect that holiday's theme, and I usually dress up in a costume to personally deliver the bags to the children. The staff at Johns Hopkins has also found that keeping a few extra Love Boxes in the

---

*To learn more about incorporation, see pp. 144–145.

Megan Leaf

pediatric emergency room can do wonders to calm any children who are being treated there.

I first got the idea to create Love Boxes when I had to stay overnight at the Children's Center for testing. Before that, I'd only visited for doctors' appointments, and I hadn't realized how monotonous staying in the hospital could be. When children stay overnight, their entertainment depends on when the toy room is open and when they can borrow toys. My idea was to give young patients something to do and play with, and even take home with them.

When I first began making the Love Boxes, I had very limited resources. I depended on empty shoe boxes from shoe stores for the packaging, and on friends, family, and my 4-H club for donations of toys to fill the boxes. After delivering the Love Boxes for a few months, my enterprise became a Valentine's Day story in local newspapers and on television. Soon I began receiving letters and checks in the mail from people who had seen and/or read about my business and wanted to help.

Each Christmas, I send out Christmas cards and a small newsletter about what Love Box and I have accomplished in the past year to everyone who has sent or given me a donation. I'm so grateful to everyone who has helped me to continue making the Love Boxes. The money I've received, and continue to receive, has been enough to enable me to set up a bank account; buy all new toys, games, and stuffed animals for the kids; and become an official business.

Because I've overcome the initial difficulties of affording nice things to put in the bags, running Love Box has been much easier. After I decorate the bags, I fill them with all sorts of fun things such as teddy bears, crayons, and toys. As the sole employee, I'm always busy decorating the bags, keeping inventory of my stock, and shopping around for good prices on playdough and stuffed animals. As busy as I am, making and delivering Love Boxes is still as fun and rewarding as it was when I started.

Because of my business and my dedication to it, I've been awarded some wonderful honors. I was the 1992 recipient of Maryland's Governor's Volunteer Award, and, within the past year, I've been given national scholarship money from the Pizza Hut Kids Hall of Fame, the J.C. Penney Golden Rule Award, and the Prudential Spirit of Community Award. Since 1992, I've also been featured in magazines such as *Caring People, Weekly Reader, Good Housekeeping, National Geographic World, Woman's World,* and *Exceptional Parent.*

Because of Love Box, Limited, I've been privileged to meet Maryland's current and previous governor, local newscasters with whom I've become friends, and many ill but happy kids. I've also been asked to speak before clubs, which is a source of income for me. Each club that I've spoken to has donated money to Love Box. My speeches to Kiwanis clubs, Rotary clubs, Lions clubs, and the Knights of Columbus have improved my public speaking skills and introduced me to individuals who want to help.

My nonprofit status is a little different from other businesses but involves just as much work. As the founder and sole operator of my nonprofit organization, I personally don't make any money. Yet Love Box as a company has received donations totaling over three thousand dollars. The monetary benefits I've received have come in the form of a total of twenty thousand dollars in scholarship money for my postsecondary education.

As a high school sophomore, I'm not sure what my future will involve. I plan to attend college after high school, and, in the meantime, I'll definitely keep running my business. I hope to pursue a career that will enable me to continue helping others.

Because I started Love Box when I was only ten years old, this business has become a very big and important part of my life. I started the project to help the patients at Johns Hopkins a little bit, and I had no idea that it would grow so large or give me so much in return. I'm more self-confident and have better self-esteem because of my business. But the best rewards I've received are the smiles from the kids when I hand them a bag full of toys.

My advice to other entrepreneurs is to start a business that you're really interested in and have fun with it. If you attempt something that you don't enjoy, it has very little chance of success.

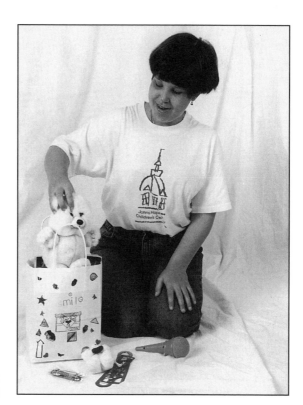

**Megan filling a
bag with toys**

Christa McHugh

Web Design

Christa McHugh, a twenty-one-year-old senior at St. Joseph's University in Philadelphia, Pennsylvania, is majoring in Information Systems. She works in the Office of Information Technology at St. Joseph's as a student intern for the vice president of information technology. In her spare time, she likes to surf, play guitar, in-line skate, and go to concerts.

Christa's mother, Arlene, is a retired real estate appraiser, and her father, Thomas, is an entrepreneur in the data processing field. He once worked on the project that designed what we know today as ATM money machines. Her sister, Alison, is sixteen years old and enjoys dance. Her family lived in the Philadelphia area for most of their lives, then moved to Tampa in 1993.

I DIDN'T BEGIN WORKING WITH COMPUTERS UNTIL I ENTERED COLLEGE. Because my freshman dormitory had network services, I had a network computer in my room. I started using email to keep in contact with my high school friends, and I learned a lot about the Internet. I soon got a job working at the school's PC Lab as a computer consultant. My employer was pleased with my work and offered me a summer job working on the Internet, researching and learning about the World Wide Web.

The university wanted to be able to use the Internet in the labs, teach it in computer workshops, and create a Web page. I was responsible for learning Hypertext Markup Language (HTML), testing new software, and finding everything the university needed to know to utilize the Web. My job led to an invitation

Christa McHugh

to sit on the St. Joseph's University World Wide Web Committee, which consisted of administrators from various departments within the university who were responsible for the design and implementation of the school's Web-based information system. I was the only student on the committee.

At the same time, I also received a job for the upcoming academic year as a resident network consultant. I was responsible for networking the students' computers in the network dormitories and providing technical support. I received free room and board and a salary of one hundred dollars a week. My work earned me appearances in the *Christian Science Monitor* and *USA Today*.

I soon started doing work on the World Wide Web for extra money. My boss knew someone who was looking for a student to design a Web site for him. She recommended me for the job to design a site advertising a line of vacuum cleaners.

From then on, via word-of-mouth, I've been designing Web sites for people as a business. I enjoy creating the sites because I get to exercise my creativity and drawing skills. Designing Web sites lets me do something creative and make money at the same time. Because of my work, I was featured in an article in *U.S. News and World Report*.

I usually charge about twenty dollars an hour to design a Web site, and the average cost for my customers is about seven hundred dollars. I've completed pages for various organizations, including financial corporations, local businesses, high schools, and university departments. I do all of the work in my dorm room. The only materials I need for my business are a computer, an image scanner, and some graphics software. It doesn't take much to learn and use the computer commands to create a Web site, but you need a creative mind to organize and present the information in a coherent and colorful way.

A Web designer must make the client (whether a company, a university, or any other organization) look good on the Web site

Christa working on her computer

because it's a form of advertising that potentially millions of people might see. My customers are sensitive to the images and words I choose to use. I usually spend ten hours designing a site and thirty hours revising and re-revising until my customer is satisfied.

I'll be graduating from college soon, and I hope to continue my work with computers in the future. I know that all of the skills I've learned from running my business will help me throughout my career.

If you're thinking about starting your own business, I have some advice for you. First, go out and try lots of new things while you're young. Take chances, take risks. Secondly, it's okay if you fail once in a while because a failure can be a learning experience. When you're young, it's easier to bounce back from a mistake. Being a risk-taker and staying positive will help you to be the best entrepreneur you can be!

Victoria Groves

Letter Perfect

Victoria Groves, eighteen, is a freshman at the University of
Massachusetts at Amherst, studying communications and journalism.
Her hometown is Chelmsford, Massachusetts, where she has lived all
of her life. Her mother, Maureen, is a secretary; her father, Eric, is a
computer coordinator at a high school. Victoria has a brother, Tom,
who's twelve.

Throughout high school, Victoria was active in student council,
serving as president of her high school student council as well as
president of the Northeastern Massachusetts Association of Student
Councils. Active in Distributive Education Clubs of America (DECA),
she traveled to the national conference in April of 1996. Victoria likes
to participate in speech competitions, travel, run, write, and read.
She traveled to England, Belgium, and France during the summer of
1996 as her state's winner of the Educational Foundation
Ambassadors Scholarship for Community Service.

IN FEBRUARY OF 1995, I WAS LUCKY ENOUGH TO BE HONORED AS A
winner of the An Income of Her Own National Teen Business Plan
Competition. I created Letter Perfect, a data processing and desktop publishing business that I run from my home. I wrote an
eight-page business plan about the services that I'd provide to my
clients, such as creating newsletters, form letters, letterheads, business cards, and menus. I projected the overhead (business
expenses that can't be charged to a certain part of the work or
product) and profits for the business, too.

Victoria Groves

When I decided to enter the competition, I wanted to create a business that would have low overhead, be flexible so I could balance it with my schoolwork, and be enjoyable. A desktop publishing business was perfect because I love working with computers, and I have all of the equipment that I need at home. In my plan, I said I would advertise to local businesses around my town and offer to format their newsletters, business cards, menus, manuscripts, contracts, form letters, etc. My expenses would consist mainly of paper and postage.

I projected that I could make over four thousand dollars in the first year. As of right now, I haven't reached that goal, but I'm working hard. It's very difficult to get clients in a field such as technology, which is extremely competitive and ever-changing. I've relied

Victoria at her computer

mainly on word-of-mouth since I haven't yet made enough money to advertise in the media.

I attended the awards ceremony at the National Association of Women Business Owners (NAWBO) annual conference in Miami in 1996, and until then I didn't know anyone who has her own business, and I hadn't had a lot of experience with businesspeople. In Miami, I met many women business owners, toured women-owned businesses in the Miami area, and participated in a panel where we discussed our business plans with local teens. I was privileged to be interviewed by several TV stations and had an article written about me in the *Lowell Sun,* my local newspaper. I was even interviewed by *Seventeen* magazine for an article on summer jobs and entrepreneurship. While in Miami, I also went to a bank and talked to some loan officers about how to borrow money to start a new business. After the conference, I was so excited about being an entrepreneur that I couldn't wait to get started.

I never imagined what an impact winning the An Income of Her Own competition would have on me. This past year, I took a management course at my high school and have become involved in DECA, which has given me the opportunity to compete nationally in a high school business competition. I keep in touch with all of the women at An Income Of Her Own and have received a subscription to *Blue Jean* magazine for teens, a membership to Women Incorporated, and gifts from businesses such as IBM, Esprit, and Wells Fargo Bank, among others.

Writing a business plan helped me to learn a lot about myself. It forced me to sort out my ideas and think about questions such as: Where will I get the money to start this business? What will make my services better than those of my competitors? Is there a need for my services in my community? What price should I charge for each service? By answering these questions, I was able to envision my business flourishing and to anticipate some of the glitches that could occur. This gave me the opportunity to iron out problems ahead of time.

I've decided that after I get out of college, I want to become very active in the field of business. Even if Letter Perfect doesn't turn out to be as perfect as I'd planned, I'm confident that whatever I set my mind to and work hard at, I can achieve. I hope that my college education, my enthusiasm, and my motivation will take me far in the business world.

Tara Church

Tree Musketeers*

Tara Church is an eighteen-year-old freshman at the University of Southern California. Tara is an honor student, and when she's not studying or working, she enjoys politics, reading and writing poetry, and art of all kinds.

Her mother, Gail, is the Executive Director of Tree Musketeers, and her father, Lee, is an air safety inspector. Tara has a twenty-one-year-old brother named Brook. She grew up in El Segundo, California, a small beach community, and she owes much of her success to the community's support of her uncommon goal of starting a nonprofit corporation. But Tara gives most of the credit to her mother, who taught her to dream big dreams and believe in them.

I REMEMBER THE DAY IN 1987 WHEN MY BROWNIE TROOP DISCUSSED the environmental consequences of using disposable dishes. The conversation wandered from the cutting down of trees to make paper products, to the landfill crisis and air pollution, to ozone depletion. Our leaders described a group that was researching the idea of people living underground if environmental damage were to render earth unlivable. I'll never forget the brief but chilling vision I had of dark, overcrowded caverns beneath the burning surface of the earth, and the echo of crying children.

Then I had an idea—we should plant a tree to help the planet. I thought that an increased population of trees would be one small

---

*If you're interested in learning more about Tree Musketeers, write to: Tree Musketeers, 136 Main St., Suite A, El Segundo, CA 90245-3800.

Tara Church

way of helping the environment, and that if young people took the lead, others might follow. On May 9, 1987, I planted Marcie the Marvelous Tree with my Girl Scout troop. After the planting, I marveled at the simplicity of the act and the amazing potential of a single tree.

That day, El Segundo became the birthplace of the youth environmental movement called Tree Musketeers. Although starting a nationwide organization wasn't in our thoughts at the time, we took the first step toward forming one when we embraced a collective vision. This vision was of children all over the world planting trees, fostering social change, and uniting to take action against environmental destruction.

The organization grew as a result of public demand, and our projects became larger. As word spread of our youth-led activities,

Tara *(back row, left)* helping children to plant a tree

calls came from all corners of the country, with people asking how they could start their own groups. We set up a hotline and formed a speakers' bureau. We even incorporated.* Unlike most youth groups, we organized Tree Musketeers as a tax-exempt, nonprofit corporation that would continue to be administered by kids. This required us to define our mission, meaning the kind of activities our organization would conduct and how we would go about bringing our vision to reality.

We decided that our mission was to empower youth to provide environmental leadership through innovative action and through educational programs that motivate other young people to become partners in a united youth movement. Our belief is that, neighborhood by neighborhood, kids can save the earth.

As the organization grew, our path became bumpy and littered with roadblocks. The first major obstacle was establishing a

---

*To learn more about incorporation, see pp. 144–145.

corporation that left kids in charge. There were no bylaws (rules adopted by an organization on how members should be governed and how the organization should be run) that we could copy. So an attorney helped us to craft the legal documents and the policy to solve this problem. It then took the world a while to grow accustomed to kids leading an organization. The media and business communities were inclined to look right past us and to converse with our adult partners. In response, we decided that only *kids* could publicly represent Tree Musketeers. This meant that we had to be well-prepared for all business meetings and media interviews. When the media asked questions of our adult partners, they purposely redirected the questions to us.

One major difficulty remains with us today: We've realized that, in general, there's a bias against youth-led programs. Many people wonder why we didn't just join an adult environmental organization, instead of starting our own. In addition, people often don't see that we have the same financial needs as adult-sponsored groups. Nevertheless, Tree Musketeers managed to grow from a neighborhood tree-planting project to a national organization in just five years on 100 percent volunteer power, almost no money, and the tenacity of kids.

Tree Musketeers has worked hard to make people more aware of the need to protect trees and the environment. Some of our successes have been to return Arbor Day to our local calendar, publish a regular newspaper column, persuade merchants to carry environmentally friendly products, start school programs focusing on the environment, and "adopt out" thousands of homeless baby trees to loving kids. We've also participated in the planting of hundreds more trees, led water conservation efforts that have kept our landscape alive, and solicited environmental resolutions from local businesses and residents. Thanks to Tree Musketeers, a weed-infested median strip between El Segundo and the Los Angeles Airport became a beautiful park-like grove that's part of our 700-tree pollution barrier around the city.

Our other activities have included producing *Tree Stumpers,* an environmental quiz show for community cable TV; chairing the committee that drafted the city's waste management plan; and opening the community's first recycling center. El Segundo became the "laboratory" in which we developed, documented, and packaged a Hometown Forests program as an action kit that we've made available to other towns interested in improving their landscape. With partner groups, we host national and regional youth summits twice a year, and we provide editorial content for *Grassroots Youth* magazine, an international publication for the entire youth movement. Leadership, Empowerment, and Action Development (LEAD) is our newest program, in which kids in fifth to eighth grade lead a three-month environmental project.

Although I was one of the founders and have remained a primary leader all these years, Tree Musketeers has been a success due to the collective efforts of my peers, adult supporters, financial partners, and various levels of government. Tree Musketeers has grown tremendously since its founding, and nine staff members (mostly youth) are now needed for running the day-to-day operations. Yet the organization remains primarily volunteer-driven, with some

Tara leading a workshop on curbside recycling

16,000 hours donated annually. Our work has been widely honored, and we received the Volunteer Action Award from President Clinton in a Rose Garden ceremony on Earth Day in 1994.

Empowering other youth has been the driving force behind my work. Starting and running this organization has helped me to master working with a group, project management, and organizational development. Tree Musketeers has also given me the opportunity to use and improve my written and spoken communication skills. I've also learned more than I ever wanted to know about budgeting. I know I've really made a difference in the lives of young people; letters from kids all over the world are among my most treasured possessions.

People sometimes express the observation that I "never really had a childhood." But that's not true. I simply chose to experience my childhood in a different way. If I could go back ten years, I'd do the same thing again, and probably work a little harder!

Most young entrepreneurs are paid back for their dedication with money. In the nonprofit world, our reward is progress toward the mission, and I'm a rich person for that.

Nicole Koneffko

Santa's Place

Nineteen-year-old Nicole Koneffko graduated in 1996 from Belle Vernon High School in Belle Vernon, Pennsylvania. During her junior year in high school, she started her business, Santa's Place, with her business partner and boyfriend, Michael Mendicino.

As a senior, Nicole became a part-time student at Duquesne University in Pittsburgh, where she now attends full-time to pursue her Bachelor's degree in Business Administration and Entrepreneurial Studies. Nicole enjoys interior decorating, video production, and graphic design, as well as going out with her friends or seeing a good movie. Her parents, Diane (a schoolteacher and owner of a print shop) and Dennis (the owner of an engineering company), and her brother, Zach (age seventeen), describe Nicole as motivated and hard-working. These traits have helped Nicole to create a thriving business.

SINCE MY DAYS OF SELLING LEMONADE ON THE CORNER, I'VE ALWAYS had an entrepreneurial spirit. I was the kid who took charge (you know the type—there's one at every lemonade stand!). I was the one setting the prices and attracting the customers. Even then, my goal was to own a business.

It's often said that entrepreneurs are motivated and eager people. In my case, this is definitely true. By the time I reached my teens, I was anxious to unleash my passion for business.

With my boyfriend, I started Santa's Place at age sixteen. Our business provides children with a scheduled visit from Santa Claus and one of his elves. The kids who are paid a visit receive a personalized letter from the North Pole that mentions a certain night when

Nicole Koneffko

Santa will be in their neighborhood. On that night, Santa and the elf appear outside of the children's homes to check up on who's "naughty or nice." Santa also stops in each home to visit with the children and to deliver a special personalized ornament. Then, in a flash, Santa disappears into the night.

I began planning the business in October of 1994. Once I had developed the idea and worked out the details, it was time to market it. I designed a brochure and handed it to parents on conference days at the local schools. I made signs and hung them in stores. By far, the most effective (and least expensive!) advertising came from articles in the newspaper, which told the story of two teenagers running a business. After that, the calls poured in. By mid-November, nearly all of December was completely booked! On some nights, Santa was scheduled to make as many as ten visits.

When December came, it was time to put Santa into action. I played the elf and my boyfriend played Santa Claus. On the first night, I was both nervous and excited. We made three visits that night, and all of them seemed to go well. The children were thrilled, and their parents were equally pleased.

However, not all nights went so smoothly. Unclear directions to homes were a common problem. Bad weather also created difficulties. We even had a few mischievous children snap Santa's beard. At times, it was difficult to manage a full day of school, ten Santa visits, and a night of homework.

Even through the tough times, I enjoyed the visits. I really like kids, and each visit was a lot of fun. When I look back, what I remember most are the good times. I believe that liking what you do is crucial to running a strong business.

Quality is really the key to the success of Santa's Place. One of my goals has been to provide children with memories that will never be forgotten. Every detail of the visit is magical, from the glitter dust on the child's letter to the twinkle in Santa's eye. A second goal with my business is affordability. At only fifteen dollars a visit, most parents can afford my services. For those who can't, a third goal is charity. Santa's Place spends time each season visiting less fortunate children in the community, as well as children in local hospitals. Santa's Place is truly a part of the holiday spirit.

The first year of business was even more successful than I had predicted it would be. Not only did the business do well financially, but the customers seemed to be extremely satisfied. It was rewarding to receive letters and calls of thanks from parents. Many customers who knew of my young age were even more supportive because of it. Perhaps the best compliments, however, have come when customers expressed that they had no idea that a young person owned the company. Their words made me feel more confident about my ability to run a business and to compete with adults.

My family has been very supportive of my goals and of my business. My father is an entrepreneur—maybe I inherited some of his characteristics. Together, we went to some small business seminars. I also found support in other places. Through the gifted program at my high school, I learned about several business plan competitions. I entered each of them with the plan for Santa's Place.

In early January of 1995, I got news from the first contest, which was sponsored by An Income of Her Own. I had won! The prize was a trip to Washington, D.C., and North Carolina with six other winners to attend the National Association of Women Business Owners (NAWBO) Economic Summit. The trip was wonderful. We toured the capital, and I had a good time with the other winners, who were very impressive.

Best of all, I had a chance to meet a lot of remarkable businesswomen. The encouragement and support of these business leaders was incredible. When we received our awards at the luncheon, we got a standing ovation. I was overwhelmed, amazed, and satisfied that my business efforts could attract so much support from so many important women.

Not long after I returned from my trip, I learned that I had won a second business plan competition sponsored by Seton Hill College. As my prize, I attended Camp Entrepreneur that summer. The camp was a weeklong experience in starting and running a business. Once

Michael *(left)* and Nicole dressed for a Santa visit

again, I received tremendous support and encouragement. I learned so much that week and had a lot of fun.

Santa's Place had another successful season in 1995. However, now that my boyfriend and I have graduated from high school and have gone on to college, the business has come to a temporary halt. I believe that to become the best businesswoman I can be, I need an education. In fact, a college education is the best possible investment I can make in my business.

I know that my business experience has brought a lot to my college education. I've gained a good deal of practical knowledge that's applicable in many of my classes. I've also come to appreciate the usefulness of what I learn by applying it to the real-world situation of my business.

After college, I plan to pursue my entrepreneurial dreams. I haven't yet decided what path I'll follow. Perhaps I'll continue Santa's Place on a larger scale, or perhaps I'll take a new direction. I do know that I'll be running my own business and that I'll love what I'm doing.

I've gained so much from my experiences over the past few years. I've learned that being young and female can be two wonderful entrepreneurial ingredients. Yes, youth can be an obstacle when it comes to being taken seriously; however, behind every hurdle is an opportunity. Youth *can* be an advantage. In my situation, being so young brought attention to my business. It became a great marketing tool. Youth also has another advantage: little to lose. It's a lot easier to take risks when a house, a family, and a secure job aren't on the line. I've also found that being female can be advantageous. Women are excellent at forming support networks. I've received tremendous support from women as I've worked to build my business.

The best advice I can give to other business owners, future entrepreneurs, or anyone in general is this: The road less traveled is often the most rewarding and satisfying road of all. In my own experience, my proudest accomplishments are the ones that took the most courage and the most heart to achieve. Don't be afraid to take a risk, and always follow your dreams!

Service Businesses

Questions to Think About, Ideas to Try

1. Look around your home, school, and community—are there services that would make your life easier or more comfortable? What services might help very young children, adults, or the elderly in your area? This could be the starting point for your service business. Find out what you or other people need, then think of a way to provide such a service.

2. Some of the girls in this book have faced the challenge of being told that they're too young to run a business. How would you respond to this attitude? What can you do to overcome any obstacles that your age might present? Other girls in the book have found that youth can be an advantage when running a business. What are some of the positive aspects of youth-led businesses?

3. Volunteer experiences can help you to gain business, service, and leadership skills. Find opportunities for volunteering in your community—at a hospital, a nursing home, a school, a day-care center, or a community recreation program. Keep notes about your experiences and how they might help you to run a business.

4. Running any type of business requires hard work and time-management skills. To maintain a healthy balance of activities in your life while running a successful business, you'll need to set up a schedule and stick to it. First, make a chart of your

123

business duties, daily activities, and chores, then figure out how much time each one takes. (TIP: Be sure to include eating and sleeping in your time-management chart!) Do you have enough time in the day to do it all? Next, prioritize the items on your list. If you find that you hardly have enough time to get the important things done, you may need to eliminate an activity or come up with a way to handle tasks more efficiently. Modify your schedule as often as needed.

5. Make a list of some of the people in your community who own successful service businesses. Set up appointments to talk with them about their business goals, why and how they got started, advice they may have for you, and roadblocks they've encountered. Take notes during the interview, or ask the individual if it would be okay to tape record the conversation so you can review it whenever you'd like. If you really connect with one of these people, ask him or her to be your mentor. A mentor can offer advice, encouragement, ideas, and help.

6. As you try to put together your own business plan, don't be afraid to ask other people for input and advice. Contact a few business owners or a small business administration office and say that you'd like some information on developing a plan for your service business. Perhaps you could see a sample of a real plan, which might give you some creative ideas. Ask those who've helped you if they would be willing to review your plan once you've completed it.

7. One thing that many of the girls in this book hold in common, besides entrepreneurship, is persistence. Are you persistent? Do you pursue your goals despite any obstacles? Keep in mind the old saying "If at first you don't succeed, try, try again" because it really works! Create your own saying about persistence, and post it in your room, your business, your locker, or any other place where you'll see it each day.

8. Many of the entrepreneurs in this book have taken classes, attended lectures and/or conferences, gone to camps, etc., to improve their business skills. What opportunities could you take advantage of to improve your business skills? For further ideas, take a look at some books about entrepreneurship and business (for resources, see pp. 156–159 and pp. 165–169).

9. Investigate the differences in establishing a nonprofit vs. a for-profit business. Make a list of the advantages and disadvantages of each to help you determine which type of business to start.

10. One advantage of running a service business is that it may cost you very little to get started, since you're probably not manufacturing a product (although some service businesses do feature related products). One disadvantage is that the service you provide may involve tasks that most people wouldn't consider much fun. Make a list of the pros and cons to decide if the service business you've chosen is right for you.

11. Once you've decided on the type of service business to try, check out the competition. Look in the Yellow Pages to find similar businesses in your area and find out how much they charge for their services. If there are no similar businesses in your area, GREAT! If the competition is stiff, see if you can provide better service and charge less money so customers will come to you.

12. If you don't think you have time to run a business year-round, a seasonal business may be just the thing for you. Perhaps you could run the business during the summer when you're out of school, or perhaps you could provide services that are needed during a certain season only (such as snow shoveling, holiday gift wrapping, leaf raking, etc.).

13. If you need a loan to get your business started, make a list of possible sources (a bank, a savings and loan, investors, family or friends, a grant, and so on). What are the pros and cons of each? Find out how much money you'll really need and write up a strong business plan to show potential lenders. Make a plan for how and when you'll pay back the money.

Part Two

How to Be an Entrepreneur

Getting Started

N OW THAT YOU'VE READ ABOUT GIRLS AND YOUNG WOMEN STARTING and running their own businesses, you may want to become an entrepreneur, too. People of *all* ages can find success in the business world. In fact, research shows that the average age of entrepreneurs has been shifting downward since the early 1960s. Of the fourteen million small businesses in the United States, 22 percent are run by people under the age of thirty-five.

Running a business is hard work, but it has many benefits. The payoffs of entrepreneurship include:

- the satisfaction of putting your own ideas into action
- a way to share your creative talents with others
- control of your future
- the ability to be your own boss and to set your own hours
- increased knowledge and skills (managing your time and money, for example)
- the freedom to do something you love
- a sense of fulfillment
- a chance to make your own contribution to the world
- improved communication skills (written and oral)
- increased confidence
- the opportunity to make your own choices and decisions
- financial independence
- a way to help other people to lead better lives.

If running a business sounds like what you really want to do, think about whether you "have what it takes" for this kind of enterprise.

Some entrepreneurs aren't successful—not because they don't know how to run a business, but because they don't understand their own strengths and weaknesses. The most successful entrepreneurs generally have the following strengths:

- self-confidence
- creativity
- a willingness to take risks
- patience
- ambition
- determination
- optimism
- persistence
- desire to achieve
- dependability
- good communication skills
- self-discipline
- ability to set and reach for goals
- motivation
- commitment.

Don't worry—very few people have *all* of these qualities. But the traits that characterize successful entrepreneurs generally include a positive outlook, high energy, and an I-can-do-it attitude. Entrepreneurs are willing to work hard because they believe that what they're doing is important and that they can make a difference in the world. They are self-starters. And they finish what they start.

If you think you have some or many of the traits described above, you're probably well on your way to becoming a successful entrepreneur. Even if you don't have many of these qualities, you can develop them. Start by looking at the above list and deciding which traits describe you and which ones don't. Once you've figured out what your weaknesses are, you can find ways to overcome them. For example, you could sharpen your communication skills by taking a writing or speech class. Or learn to set goals and stick to them by making lists of your short-term and long-term goals and consulting the lists often to remain focused. Stay optimistic by replacing negative thoughts ("I can't do it, so why should I try?") with positive ones ("I can do anything I set my mind to, so I'll keep trying until I succeed!").

It might also help to find other entrepreneurs who can act as role models for you. Think of business owners in your community whom you'd like to get to know, then seek them out. Call or write to them, and ask if they'd be willing to take the time to talk to you about how they got their start. Learn about their successes, the obstacles they overcame, and the qualities that have helped them in business and in life. If you can't talk to people personally, read about them. Go to the library to find business magazines, books about entrepreneurs, or newspaper articles about any local businesspeople who've experienced success (see pp. 156–159 and 165–169 for resource ideas). Browse the World Wide Web for sites about businesses or entrepreneurs that you admire.

As you take these steps, write about your experiences in your Business Notebook. This is a great place to collect and record your thoughts, your dreams, your activities, and your ideas.

So, how do you develop your ideas. . . ?

Getting Ideas

Every business starts as a thought in the mind of the entrepreneur. So give yourself plenty of time, space, and freedom to come up with lots of ideas. Remember that ideas for your business may fall into two general groups—a product business or a service business. Do you have a product to sell or a service to offer? Maybe some combination of both? Developing the idea for your business is a critical step. Take your time and weigh your options.

Step One: Brainstorming All Possibilities

When brainstorming, let the ideas flow! Don't hold back. Consider anything and everything, and write all of your ideas down. You don't have to show your list to anyone if you don't want to, so don't be afraid to write something that you may think is a little off-the-wall. Your Business Notebook is a good place for your brainstorming list.

As you brainstorm, keep in mind that the point of the process is *quantity* over *quality*. The more ideas you have to start with, the more likely you'll be to find at least one idea that works.

You can use the following questions as a guide when brainstorming. Respond to the questions yourself, then ask your friends and family members to respond to them. You could even pose some of the questions to people in chat rooms on the Internet, but be careful to protect your ideas, too!

1. What kinds of things do people dislike doing for themselves?

2. What kinds of things are people too busy to do for themselves?

3. What kinds of products would I like to see improved?

4. How can I help people to save time?

5. How can I help people to save money?

6. What kinds of products or services would make life easier?

7. How do people like to spend their time?

8. What kinds of services might be needed by certain groups of people (such as children, teenagers, adults, the elderly)?

9. What kinds of products might appeal to certain groups of people (such as children, teenagers, adults, the elderly)?

10. What products/services could help people in my community, state, or nation?

You can generate other ideas through research. Take a look at the *Wall Street Journal* to find interesting information about businesses, entrepreneurs, and products that sell. Telephone books are another source of information for products and services. Go to your local library to examine the Yellow Pages of telephone books from several places—they're a good springboard for ideas.

Remember to record every idea in your Business Notebook. This will help you to stay organized. Reading over your lists periodically can help spark *even more* ideas.

Step Two: Matching Business Ideas with You

Once you've collected lots of business ideas, it's time to narrow down your list and seriously consider which ideas are best for you. Many of the girls and young women in this book said that they *love* their work, which is why they're successful. It's very important to match your personal interests and talents with your business idea. This will offer you the greatest potential for satisfaction and success as a young entrepreneur. Ask yourself the following questions:

What are my passions in life?

- animals?
- children?
- sports?
- nature?
- computers?
- music?
- the environment?
- art?
- pottery?
- jewelry?
- movies?

How do I like to spend my time?

- exercising?
- playing music?
- cooking?
- making crafts?
- organizing/cleaning things?
- painting?
- working on the computer?

- being with other people?

- being outdoors?

- taking photographs?

- reading?

- sewing?

- entertaining others/planning events or parties?

- shooting videos?

- repairing things?

- gardening?

After thinking about what you love to do and how you enjoy spending your time, ask yourself this question: What am I good at? Chances are, you're beginning to have a clear idea of your favorite activities and your talents and interests.

Now that you know which activities best suit you, figure out how you can turn your passion into a business idea. For example, if you love writing and working on the computer, you could consider starting a desktop publishing business. If you love to organize special events, you could plan children's birthday parties or other celebrations. If you enjoy nature and the outdoors, you could garden for people in your community or start an environmental organization. The possibilities are endless.

The more you know about yourself, the better job you'll do of determining the business that's right for you. Focus on a business that will allow you to use your strengths and to make the most of your special talents.

Step Three: Determining the Feasibility of the Idea

While developing your business idea, it's important to analyze its *feasibility*. This process gives you the chance to look at the facts and determine if it's possible to accomplish what you're setting out to do. In other words: Will the idea work?

Use the following questions to determine the feasibility of your idea:

1. Is it legal?
2. Is it practical?
3. Is there a demand for this product or service in my community?
4. Do I have the knowledge and skills needed to implement this idea?
5. Do I have or can I find enough money to get started?
6. Do I have or can I find the necessary space and equipment?
7. What permits, licenses, insurance, and/or legal services will I need?
8. How much of my time will it take? Do I *have* the time?
9. What am I risking to pursue this idea?
10. Who are my competitors?

The answers to these questions will help you to focus and will guide you in preparing a well-researched business plan. You can find the answers to some of these questions by using your public library, your local chamber of commerce, or the county courthouse, or by consulting with other business owners and/or an attorney.

Now you're ready to move on to another creative part of becoming an entrepreneur—naming your business.

Naming Your Business

Many experts say that naming your business is one of the most important steps in winning customers. When choosing a name, consider what's appropriate for the type of business you have and the kind of customer you want to attract. A business name can tell the customer about the type of product or service you provide (Babysitting by the Hour, Creative T-shirts), who owns the business (Blair's Bakery), or the location of the business (Main Street Crafts).

Your business name represents you and the unique product or service you have to offer. It's your customers' first impression, and first impressions *are* important.

To find a name for your business, brainstorm a list of words and phrases that relate to your business idea. Read through the list and see if anything stands out. Play with the words and phrases until you come up with several ideas that work.

Next, research the names of businesses that already exist to make sure the name you selected is unique. Check carefully at your library, in your local telephone books, or at the county clerk's office to be sure that the name isn't taken. You may want to ask a librarian to help you with this process.

Keep the name of your business short and simple so people can remember it. You may want to try a unique twist for the name to make it more interesting or appealing. The bottom line is: *Choose a name that will help you sell your product or service.* You can determine which business name is most popular by testing possible ideas with family members, friends, and potential customers before you make your final decision.

Once you've settled on a name, you must file a Doing Business As (DBA) form at the county clerk's office. The registration fee usually ranges from five to thirty dollars. Filing this form allows you to reserve your business name so no one else in the county can use it. Business registrations expire over a period of time (approximately four years or less), so you'll need to reapply. Keep a copy of this form for the bank if you plan to open an account under the name of your business.

Writing Your Business Plan

It's not enough just to have a good idea and a name for your product or service. The business plan is *critical* to your success as an entrepreneur. Many entrepreneurs like action, so they jump in and start their business immediately. But the most effective entrepreneurs delay the excitement of getting started so they can prepare a strong foundation for their business.

The business plan is the road map that you'll follow as you chart the course of your business. In your business plan, you'll need to clearly describe your business and to look at it from all sides—marketing, operations, and finance. The plan, which you'll show to potential investors and any officials involved in the legal side of your business, is a good way for you to look at the details and facts before starting your business.

Because potential investors will use your business plan to make decisions about the amount of money they wish to lend, it must convey a sense of originality, enthusiasm, and optimism. They'll carefully analyze several factors: the soundness of the idea, your talent and reliability, the amount of cash flow needed, your collateral (something you own that's of equal value to the loan), and the amount of the financial contribution you've committed to the project. Your business plan is one of the most important investments *you* can make in your own business, so take the time to write the best plan possible.

Your business plan may also be read by people *inside* of the business (partners and employees, for example). So it must provide a detailed picture of every aspect of the business and how the pieces all fit together. You and your partners/employees can refer to the plan periodically to make sure that your business stays on course.

You can also use your business plan as a way of measuring the performance of the business over time. Experts recommend that you develop the plan for a three- to five-year time span and that you make projections as to how you expect the business to grow.

Create a business plan that is thoughtful and professional. A strong business plan is:

- easy to understand
- well organized
- interesting (include graphics)
- serious
- realistic
- well written
- brief but thorough.

A weak business plan is:

- vague
- hard to follow
- dull
- simplistic
- overstated
- full of errors
- long-winded.

To make sure your business plan reads well and looks professional, find someone who can help you to develop it. Perhaps a business friend or mentor could review the plan and give you some feedback. Ask your parents or your friends to honestly critique the plan and to offer any helpful comments or suggestions. If you know a writer or skilled proofreader, ask that individual to look over your plan. In exchange for their work, you might offer any people who help you a favor in return.

Remember that there isn't just *one* right way to write a business plan, but some components are absolutely necessary. On pages 139–141, you'll find an outline of a standard business plan and descriptions of each key part. Use the outline as a step-by-step guide to writing your own business plan. For more ideas, do some research at your local library or talk with business owners in your community.

The Parts of a Business Plan

I. Executive Summary

The executive summary is a condensed version of the entire business plan. It must capture the interest of the reader *immediately* and must highlight the basics of each part of the plan. It's best to write the executive summary after the rest of the plan has been completed.

II. General Description of the Business Idea

This part of the plan describes the type of business and its basic activities. Include information about what you hope to achieve.

III. Products and Services

This section includes a simple description of the product or service you plan to provide. You can include photographs, drawings, or diagrams. Focus on what makes your product or service appealing. What are its unique features? How did you develop it? How do you expect it to progress over time?

IV. Marketing Plan

The marketing plan explains how the business will make money (if the business is for-profit), how it will appeal to consumers, and how the business will succeed. Here's your opportunity to really sell your business! This section of your plan must be positive and persuasive. The following points can serve as a guide:

A. Describe the demand for your product or service.

B. Define your market. Who might want your product or service? Why might they want it? Where are these potential customers located?

C. Describe your competition and other influences that may affect your business.

D. Give a detailed description of your marketing strategies. How will your product or service be distributed? Packaged?

Advertised? Promoted? Priced? What is your market in different locations? What strategies will you use to get people interested in your product/service? How will you advertise? How much time and money will your marketing strategies take?

E. Give the results of any market research you've conducted related to the product. Have you used focus groups (panels of people who discuss your project) to develop your business idea? Have you tested your product or service with various groups of people? Have you sampled the opinions of potential customers?

F. Predict your general sales over a specific time period (monthly, quarterly). You may want to organize your customers into categories such as children, teens, adults, the elderly, etc.

G. Give any available research or evidence that supports the need for your product or service (industry studies, research articles, letters of support from various groups or industries, etc.).

V. Operational Plan

The operational plan describes how the product or service will be created and gives you the chance to work out any problems on paper *before* starting the business. How will you make your product? How will you offer your service? What kind of location or space do you need to make the product or to provide the service? What equipment do you need? Materials? Labor?

VI. Financial Plan

The purpose of the financial plan is to show how you expect your business to succeed financially. You can discuss your business expenses, your projected income, and your method of bookkeeping. Make sure that your information is accurate and that your financial plan matches all of the details given in the entire business plan. For example, if you describe an expensive advertising campaign in the marketing plan section, the expenses and income of the campaign must be shown in your financial plan. The following points may guide you:

A. Estimate your expenses. What are your direct material costs (supplies, equipment, etc.)? What are your direct labor costs or the wages you'll need to pay your employees? What are your overhead expenses (rent, gas, electricity, phone, packing, shipping, advertising, postage, etc.)? What taxes will you have to pay? Keep in mind that some expenses are fixed and will stay the same each month. Other costs will go up and down, depending on the activity level of your business. If possible, calculate the costs per item produced or per service rendered.

B. Estimate your income. What is your selling price per item or per service? How much do you have to sell to break even? What are your sales goals? What do you think your sales will be per month? Per quarter? Per year? For the next five years? How will you maintain a positive cash flow?

C. Determine an organized and accurate bookkeeping system. Although this process may be tedious, it can save time and allow you to run a more effective business. What type of bookkeeping system will you use? What forms do you need?

D. Make the loan request. How much money do you need to borrow and how will it be used? What is your plan for repaying the loan? What can you offer as collateral? What is your credit history? From whom have you borrowed money in the past? Did you repay it on time? Give the names of at least five credit references (people or institutions you've borrowed money from), their addresses and phone numbers, the amount of the loans, and when they were repaid.

VII. Appendix

In the appendix, you should include copies of any letters of support or other evidence of support for the business. Be sure to include copies of your licenses and permits.

VIII. Concluding Statement

Offer a concluding statement that adds one final *punch* to your business plan. The statement should be positive and enthusiastic.

When you feel confident that your business plan is in the best possible shape, make an appointment to discuss it with your banker or other potential lenders. Practice making the oral presentation in front of your family and friends before the real presentation so that you look, feel, and act confident.

Keep your business plan in an easily accessible place, not hidden away on a shelf collecting dust. The plan should always be in the front of your mind as you proceed with your business.

Another good reason for having your business plan in a handy place is that you can use the plan as a way to check the progress of your business. Periodically, you should take a look at your plan and decide if you're meeting your original marketing and financial goals. If you aren't meeting your goals, figure out why. What new strategies might help you to get back on track? Consult with other business owners or a mentor who can give you some support and advice. Be sure to modify your plan as your business grows.

Understanding Legal Issues

It's essential for entrepreneurs to have a clear understanding of all of the legal requirements for starting and running a business. Regulations are imposed by federal, state, county, and city governments. State laws differ, and many cities have their own special requirements for retail and service businesses. While there are no particular laws that apply to *all* types of businesses in *all* locations, the following information may help you to make sense of the most common laws and regulations for entrepreneurs. You may want to seek advice from a lawyer.

Contracts

Start by investigating your state's laws regarding your right to sign a contract (an agreement to do something for someone in exchange for something else). A contract may be an informal verbal agreement or a written document. For example, when you babysit or wash cars in the neighborhood for money, you usually have an informal agreement that when the work is done payment is due. A written contract, on the other hand, is formally signed by individuals or by businesses. Check your state laws to find out whether you can sign a contract. You may have to have an adult cosigner. This person assumes responsibility if you break the contract or can't fulfill its terms.

In many states, a contract with a child is voidable, meaning that the child isn't obligated to uphold the contract. Potential customers who are aware of this law may not want to do business with a young person. Some states have consequences for a child who backs out of a contract, but other states don't.

Right to Income

You may also want to examine laws pertaining to your right to your earnings. Because your parents have the responsibility to provide for you, they also have what is known as the right to income. This means that, by law, your parents are allowed to take the money you earn. The right-to-income rule applies unless the parent and child make other arrangements, in a written or implied agreement. If you've reached the age of majority (eighteen in most states), the rule no longer applies.

If you do have the right to keep what you earn, you'll probably want to open a bank account. Some banks offer special savings programs to students, or they waive their monthly service fees for minors with accounts. Some banks require minors to have a parent's consent to open the account and to withdraw or deposit money. Check the laws of your state or call a local bank to ask about its policy.

Social Security Number

You must have your own Social Security Number (SSN) in order to run your own business (or to work for someone else). You most likely received a Social Security card at birth, so ask your parents for your number. Once you have your SSN, you may register your business with the county clerk. Ask your county officials if you need to get a special license or permit to run your business.

Patents, Trademarks, and Copyrights

A patent, trademark, or copyright may be necessary to protect your business. A patent keeps others from manufacturing, using, or selling a product for a certain number of years. You can patent anything that someone can make, as well as the process for making it. You can't patent an idea or a suggestion.

A trademark is a word, phrase, symbol, or design that identifies the source of goods or services. If you're planning to use a special logo or phrase for your business, you may need a trademark.

A copyright is protection for an original artistic or literary work. For more information, write to the U.S. Government Printing Office and ask for the booklets pertaining to patents, trademarks, and copyrights. The office charges a fee for this booklet. Write to:

U.S. Government Printing Office
Superintendent of Documents
Mail stop: SSOP
Washington, D.C. 20402-9328

Your Business Structure

You must decide to operate your business as a sole proprietorship, a general partnership, or a corporation. A sole proprietorship has only one owner who makes all of the decisions and receives all of the profits. It's the simplest and least expensive business structure to operate. The main disadvantage of this business structure is that the owner bears all of the responsibility.

A general partnership is formed when two or more people agree to share ownership and, sometimes, the management of a business. The partnership allows the partners to help each other with decision making, start-up money, and other resources. The main disadvantage of a partnership is that conflicts may arise from differences in opinion between partners. If you choose this type of structure for your business, you should get the help of an attorney to establish a legal agreement between you and your partner.

A corporation is a body formed and authorized by law to act as a single person, with its own rights, privileges, and duties. Corporations have a status of their own, independent of the owner or investors. To incorporate, one, two, or three people (depending on state rules) organize and become officials in the new corporation. Establishing and running a corporation can be costly, requires a lot of paperwork, and is dependent on special laws and regulations. Think carefully about the structure that's right for you and your business.

If you plan to hire any employees, federal and state labor laws/regulations may apply to your business. Employers who hire even one employee must obtain an employee identification number and a state unemployment tax number. Applications for these numbers may be obtained from the Internal Revenue Service (IRS). The toll-free telephone number for the IRS is 1-800-829-1040.

Taxes

Unless you plan to start a nonprofit business, you may have to pay taxes. If you earn *any* amount of money throughout the year, you're likely to pay a tax to either the state or federal government, or both.

You may have to file a 1040 tax return, a Social Security tax form (Schedule SE), and a Profit Or Loss from Business form (Schedule C). Look in a tax form instruction booklet to find out which taxes apply to your business. You can find the booklets at government offices, banks, post offices, and libraries. Because the forms can be complicated, ask your parents or a tax professional for help.

Another type of tax that may affect you is sales tax. Most states require you to collect sales tax for products you sell. Many types of service businesses, on the other hand, aren't required to collect sales tax. For more information on sales tax, contact your state tax assessor's office.

Insurance

You'll need to think about getting insurance to protect your business. Liability problems include *physical* injury (for example, someone breaks a leg at your place of business), *product* injury (someone buys a product from you and it doesn't work properly), and *personal* injury (someone suffers mentally due to something that happened related to your business). For more information on insurance coverage, you may need to contact an insurance agent.

Ten Tips for Young Entrepreneurs

The following tips may help you in starting and running your own business:

1. Treat all people honestly and fairly all of the time.

2. Set realistic goals for your business. No idea is too small. You don't want to take on too much too soon.

3. Take your time and pace yourself. Trying to expand too fast can backfire.

4. Don't expect riches. If you're thinking of starting a business for fast cash or for financial reasons only, STOP! It normally takes years of hard work before you start to see a real profit.

5. Use your time wisely. Remember to maintain a healthy balance of activities in your life.

6. Stay focused on your goals. Don't let temporary setbacks get you down.

7. Don't depend on family members and friends alone to be customers. Find customers in your community, in your state, or across the nation.

8. When interpreting detailed paperwork, don't be afraid to ask for help from an adult.

9. Be a professional. Dress neatly and be dependable, punctual, and courteous.

10. Reinvest some of your profits back into the business. Thinking long-range is a great way to ensure the continuous success of your business.

Part Three

For Further Inspiration

Women Entrepreneurs
Their Words, Stories, and History

AS YOU START YOUR OWN JOURNEY TOWARD BECOMING AN entrepreneur, it's helpful to read what women who've "been there" have to say. Following are words of wisdom offered by several of today's women entrepreneurs. All of them are familiar with the ups and downs of running their own businesses and have experienced enormous success despite obstacles. You can learn more about these business owners by researching their companies at the library or on the Internet.

As you read what they have to say, think about your own experiences in entrepreneurship. Make a poster or sign with the quotes that mean the most to you. Put it in your room, locker, or place of business to remind yourself about the experiences of other women entrepreneurs. Their words can motivate you and help you to remember why you wanted to start a business in the first place.

Who else might you turn to when you need advice, feedback, or a little inspiration?

"To be successful as an entrepreneur, you must have passion for your product or service, along with a marketing vision. You also need knowledge of your product or service, a reasonable amount of capital (double what you think you'll need), the ability to move forward with a positive attitude (even when you're almost broke and your heart is broken), and a certain amount of luck, which I believe is more timing than luck."

—**Sheila Cluff,** owner of the health and fitness spas known as the Oaks at Ojai and the Palms at Palm Springs. In 1958, with only two thousand dollars, Sheila started her spa business to promote a complete approach to health and fitness, with a focus on nourishing the body, mind, and spirit. She revolutionized the spa and health club industry and created a multimillion-dollar empire.

"When you're starting out on a new road, pay attention to the knot of fear in your stomach. It means that you're on the right track. Fear comes to tell you that you're gambling with your dreams—that you're risking big odds on your own soul's desire. This isn't always a comfortable feeling, but it is a lighthouse that will guide you to your destination."

—**Terrie M. Williams,** the Terrie Williams Agency, founded in 1988. This public relations/event planning company landed actor and comedian Eddie Murphy as its first client. Terrie's business philosophy is "To do well, you must do good." She believes in the value of the personal touch in business and in giving back to the community.

"If there's something that you want to do and you feel that you can focus and that you're serious about it, go for it. Definitely. That's why I went out on a limb—because that's where the fruit is."

—**Vera Moore,** founder of Vera Moore Cosmetics. Vera Moore was an actress in New York before she started her company. In 1979, she created her own cosmetics line featuring products especially for black women.

"Education and experience open the door, but confidence, judgment, and tenacity earn us a seat at the table."

—**Ruth M. Owades,** president and founder of Calyx & Corolla, the "flower lover's flower company." In 1989, Ruth Owades wanted to give people the opportunity to send fresh flowers to loved ones and business colleagues without having to go to a flower shop. She turned a unique idea—ship flowers directly from the growers to the customer so that the flowers are fresher and less expensive than those from a florist—into a highly successful mail-order business.

"Go for it! Set your sights high, assemble the best team you can, and don't let fear get in your way. Growing my own business, hiring my first employees, and surpassing the million dollar sales were (at the same time) the most exhilarating and the scariest things I had ever done. That was, of course, until I had over 500 employees and surpassed the fifteen million dollar mark! It never seems less scary—but it does get to be even more fun."

—**Patty DeDominic,** owner of PDQ Personnel Services, Inc., the largest woman-owned temporary and permanent staffing service in Los Angeles. She started her business in 1979 with a borrowed desk, a phone, and two thousand dollars. Annual sales are now more than fifteen million.

"If you start small and don't try to grow too fast, you'll have more time to learn. Get advice from lots of people. If you pay attention and do everything to the best of your ability, treat people honestly, and pay your bills and taxes, owning your own business can be very rewarding."

—**Annemarie Colbin,** founder of the Natural Gourmet Cookery School, the oldest natural foods cooking school in the country. Annemarie started the school in 1977 to teach vegetarian cooking and the healing power of healthy food.

"Young women must have the attitude that life is full of possibilities and that obstacles are opportunities. Dreaming about a solution to an obstacle I personally faced and taking action to make a change has been one of the most rewarding and exciting adventures I have ever experienced. Little did I know then that millions of people would enjoy a new lifestyle because of my dream."

—**Marilyn Hamilton,** CEO, Quickie Designs and Sunrise Medical. Her own challenge of living with a disability inspired Marilyn to design the Quickie electric wheelchair in 1980, revolutionizing the wheelchair industry. In addition to running the business, she plays tennis, skis, and travels the world to live her life to the fullest.

"Women have to fight harder for respect and to prove themselves capable. However, the rewards can be great if you offer a quality product or service and strive for ethics in business."

—**Kathy Bressler,** owner of Cattle Kate, founded in 1981. Cattle Kate is a successful Western-wear catalog that features clothing inspired by the hardy pioneer women of the frontier. Cattle Kate clothing is designed to reflect the quality and strength of America's frontier past.

"The first time I tried to sell Chantal at a trade show, not one buyer stopped at my tiny booth on opening day. So that night, I bought an outrageous hat. The next day, when buyers stopped to admire it, I said, 'Wouldn't you like to see my colorful cookware, too?' They looked, they bought, and the rest is history. Entrepreneurs need perseverence. If you can't do it one way, do it another."

—**Heida Thurlow,** founder of the Chantal Cookware Corporation. A mechanical engineer from Germany, Heida combined her engineering and cooking talents into a lucrative business in 1971. Chantal Cookware features colorful enamel pots and pans with see-through lids. Today, the company's sales top the ten-million-dollar mark.

"If you think you can, you can. And if you think you can't, you're right."

—**Mary Kay Ash,** founder of Mary Kay Cosmetics. In 1963, Mary Kay became a pioneer in the field of selling cosmetics door-to-door. Her sales force of trained beauty consultants offer skin-care demonstrations and makeup lessons in the home, giving customers a chance to personally try the products. Each beauty consultant earns not only a sales commission but also a chance to win prizes like Mary Kay's signature pink Cadillac. This incentive plan has helped to grow the company into a multimillion-dollar business.

"Growing a business is constant discovery. With a passionate and committed attitude, you will find the right answer."

—**Hinda Miller,** cofounder of Champion Jogbra. In 1977, few companies offered products for athletic women. Hinda pioneered the sports bra by sewing together two athletic supporters; she called her creation the Jogbra. Her revolutionary product is now featured in the permanent collections of the Smithsonian Institution and the Metropolitan Museum of Art.

"You have to make it and then continually work at it. I believe it's a cycle. Up, down, up, down, and constantly striving to be the best that you can."

—**Jennifer Paige Barclay,** founder of Blue Fish Clothing, which sells block-printed, hand-dyed, artistically designed clothes. When Jennifer was in her early twenties, she began selling her distinctive T-shirts and dresses right out of her van at craft fairs and jazz festivals. Her clothing now appears in more than 400 specialty boutiques across the country and in fine department stores, with sales exceeding ten million dollars.

"The best part about owning your own business is that all your successes are your own. However, any mistakes are your own, too!"

—**Shana Kayton,** co-owner of Statuesque (clothing for tall women) with her mother, Cheryl Levine. Founded in Davie, Florida, in 1990, Statuesque began as a shoe retailer—StatShoeEsque—and expanded into clothing for tall sizes. Due to the success of its clothing line, Statuesque has expanded to include regular sizes, too.

"Learn from each mistake, strive to be better today than yesterday, and above all, LOVE what you're doing."

—**Elizabeth Coker,** cofounder of Minco Technology Labs, a leading processor, assembler, and tester of semiconductors for the medical, military, space, and commercial industries. As a single mother with an eighth grade education, Elizabeth left the backwoods of Tennessee to start her own business in 1981. She encourages employee loyalty by offering on-site day care and free educational resources.

"Don't look back in anger . . . don't look forward in fear . . . but look around with awareness."

—**Jenny Craig,** cofounder and Vice Chairman of Jenny Craig International, established in 1983. Jenny became interested in weight management after her own struggles with weight gain and getting back into shape. Her determination to help other people led her to create a program that focuses on nutrition, exercise, weight maintenance, and personal support. Today, Jenny Craig, Inc., is one of the largest weight-management companies in the world.

"Most women don't realize the tremendous power they possess within themselves to positively influence others. My business has had struggles along the way, but I've always persevered. I stay focused on my goals, not the roadblocks. Also, it helps to have a supportive network of other professional women. The key is to use your energy and passion in positive ways, stay true to your dreams, and never give up."

—**Lane Nemeth,** the president, CEO, and founder of Discovery Toys, Inc. Lane's dream was to create a company that 1) provides educational and fun products for children, and 2) offers women the chance to build a career while staying at home with their children. In 1978, she started Discovery Toys, which now has more than 30,000 "educational consultants" who present the company's products through parent demonstrations and workshops.

Books About Entrepreneurs

In this book, you've read stories of girls and young women who are fulfilling their dreams of running a business. These girls have discovered a way to offer products and services that make a difference in people's lives. In the process, they've enriched their own lives, becoming more financially independent, more confident and professional, and more committed to making their mark on the world.

Many other women throughout the world have done the same. They have invented new products, discovered untapped markets, created unique work environments, and offered products and services especially geared toward other women or to children. They've achieved notability and have gotten the satisfaction of doing things *their* way. (Many of them have made millions, too!) These female entrepreneurs have not only changed the face of the workforce but have also served as inspiring role models for other people who want to start their own businesses. Men entrepreneurs have also had a lasting impact on the world of business. Consider Levi Strauss, Henry Ford, Sam Walton (of Wal-Mart fame), and Ben Cohen and Jerry Greenfield, who created Ben & Jerry's ice cream. Their unique products and/or services are part of many people's daily lives.

Check out the following books, which tell the stories of famous entrepreneurs and business leaders. The books, most of which are biographies, are organized by reading level so that you can find stories best suited to your age. Learn about how these entrepreneurs got started, where they got their ideas, what obstacles they have faced and overcome, how they have run their businesses, and who has helped them along the way. Perhaps their stories can inspire you to develop your talents, follow your dreams, and choose the path of entrepreneurship.

Books for Elementary Students

Aten, J., *Outstanding Women* (Columbus, OH: Good Apple, 1987).

Colman, P., *Madame C. J. Walker: Building a Business Empire* (Brookfield, CT: Millbrook Press, 1994).

Goldish, M., *Levi Strauss* (Vero Beach, FL: Rourke Enterprises, 1993).

Greenburg, K., *Ben and Jerry: Ice Cream for Everyone!* (Woodbridge, CT: Blackbirch, 1994).
— *Sam Walton* (Vero Beach, FL: Rourke Enterprises, 1993).

McKissack, P., and F. McKissack, *Madame C. J. Walker: Self-Made Millionaire* (Springfield, NJ: Enslow Publishers, 1992).

Saidman, A., *Oprah Winfrey: Media Success Story* (Minneapolis: Lerner Publications, 1990).

Toby, M., and C. Greene, *Madame C. J. Walker: Pioneer Black Businesswoman* (Chicago: Children's Press, 1995).

Van Steenwyck, E., *Levi Strauss: The Blue Jeans Man* (NY: Walker, 1988).

Books for Upper Elementary Students

Brown, G., *H. Ross Perot: Texas Billionaire* (Vero Beach, FL: Rourke Enterprises, 1993).

Buffalo, A. *Meet Oprah Winfrey* (NY: Random Books for Young Readers, 1993).

Bundels, A., *Madame C. J. Walker: Entrepreneur* (Broomall, PA: Chelsea House, 1991).

Burford, B., *Chocolate by Hershey: A Story About Milton S. Hershey* (Minneapolis: The Lerner Group, 1994).

Canadeo, A., *Ralph Lauren: Master of Fashion* (Ada, OK: Garrett Educational Corporation, 1992).

Carillo, L., *Oscar De La Renta* (Austin, TX: Raintree Steck-Vaughn, 1996).

Collins, D. R., *Pioneer Plowman: A Story About John Deere* (Minneapolis: The Lerner Group, 1990).

Cush, C., *Women Who Achieved Greatness* (Chatham, NJ: Raintree Steck-Vaughn Publishers, 1994).

Daffron, C., *Gloria Steinem* (NY: Chelsea House, 1988).

Falkof, L., *Helen Gurley Brown: The Queen of Cosmopolitan* (Ada, OK: Garrett Educational Corporation, 1992).
— *John H. Johnson: The Man from Ebony* (Ada, OK: Garrett Educational Corporation, 1992).

Greenburg, K., *Bowerman and Knight: Building the Nike Empire* (Woodbridge, CT: Blackbirch, 1995).
— *Jobs and Wozniak: Creating the Apple Computer* (Woodbridge, CT: Blackbirch, 1994).
— *Levi Strauss: Blue Jean Tycoon* (Vero Beach, FL: Rourke Enterprises, 1993).

Kendall, M. E., *Steve Wozniak: The Man Who Grew the Apple* (NY: Walker & Company, 1995).

Koopman, A., *Charles P. Lazarus: The Titan of Toys R Us* (Ada, OK: Garrett Educational Corporation, 1992).

Mayberry, J., *Business Leaders Who Built Financial Empires* (Chatham, NJ: Raintree Steck-Vaughn, 1994).

Mitchell, B., *We'll Race You, Henry: A Story About Henry Ford* (Minneapolis: The Lerner Group, 1986).

Perrone, V., *Sam Walton* (NY: Chelsea House, 1995).

Riehecky, J., *Carolina Herrera: International Fashion Designer* (Danbury, CT: Children's Press, 1991).

Spiesman, H., *Debbi Fields: The Cookie Lady* (Ada, OK: Garrett Educational Corporation, 1992).

Stefoff, R., *Mary Kay Ash: Mary Kay, A Beautiful Business* (Ada, OK: Garrett Educational Corporation, 1992).

Taylor, M., *Madame C. J. Walker: Pioneer Businesswoman* (NY: Chelsea House, 1993).

Tippins, S., *Donna Karan: Designing an American Dream* (Ada, OK: Garrett Educational Corporation, 1992).

Books for Middle School Students

French, L., *Women in Business* (Milwaukee, WI: Raintree Publishers, 1979).

Gold, R., *Steve Wozniak: A Wizard Called Woz* (Minneapolis: The Lerner Group, 1994).

Haddock, P., *Lee Iacocca: Standing Up for America* (Morristown, NJ: Silver Burdett, 1987).

Jeffrey, L.S., *Great American Businesswomen* (Springfield, NJ: Enslow Publishers, 1996).

Rozakis, L., *Mary Kay* (Vero Beach, FL: Rourke Enterprises, 1993).

Weidt, M. *Blue Jeans: A Story About Levi Strauss* (Minneapolis: Carolrhoda Books, 1990).

Young, R.G., *Phillip H. Knight: Running with Nike* (Ada, OK: Garrett Educational Corporation, 1992).
— *Sam Walton: The Giant of Wal-Mart* (Ada, OK: Garrett Educational Corporation, 1992).

Zickgraf, R., *William H. Gates: From Whiz Kid to Software King* (Ada, OK: Garrett Educational Corporation, 1992).

Books for Young Adults

Henry, S., and E. Taitz, *Gloria Steinem: One Woman's Power* (Morristown, NJ: Silver Burdett Press, 1987).

Hurwitz, S., *Careers Inside the World of Entrepreneurs* (NY: The Rosen Group, 1994).

Italia, B., *H. Ross Perot: The Man Who Woke Up America* (Minneapolis: Abdo and Daughters, 1993).

Pile, R. B., *Women Business Leaders* (Ada, OK: Garret Book Company, 1995).

A Timeline of Women Entrepreneurs

You may think that women entrepreneurs are rare, that only recently has the workforce changed to include women business owners. Actually, women throughout history have been starting and running their own businesses, from small operations to megacorporations. History is filled with examples of women who decided to *make* a job rather than just *take* one. They had the courage to do the extraordinary, and they paved the way for other female entrepreneurs. Many of them have changed history. Perhaps you can, too.

4000–3000 B.C. Women were the first sowers and collectors of seeds. As towns developed, women often became the traders in their families.

2000 B.C. Women in the Near East worked as businesswomen, importers, landowners, perfumers, and shop managers.

1000 B.C. In Crete, women worked as merchants, traders, sailors, charioteers, and hunters.

A.D. 100 Roman women worked as textile manufacturers, shopkeepers, seamstresses, and managers.

300–400 Female Greek slaves were taught specialized crafts and were given the chance to buy their freedom. Many worked as vendors, selling their craft goods.

900 Women in Tibet, Nicaragua, Melanesia, Burma, Congo, Cameroon, and Nigeria ran all or most of the trade and controlled the marketplaces.

1200 Genoan merchant Mobilia Lecavella became the wine merchant to the King of France.

1502 Lady Margaret Beaufort of England established Christ's College at Cambridge University, and in 1508, established St. John's.

1643 Goody Armitage of Massachusetts became the first woman innkeeper in the American colonies.

1702 English printer Elizabeth Mallet began publishing *The Daily Courant*, the world's first daily paper to be published by a woman.

1767 Abigail Stoneman opened the Merchant's Coffee House in Newport, Rhode Island. Between 1768 and 1774, she also opened a teahouse, boardinghouse, and ballroom.

1777 Printer Mary Catherine Goddard was commissioned to print the Declaration of Independence (the United States' first document) in her Pennsylvania print shop.

1834 Marie Tussaud opened Madame Tussaud's Wax Museum in London. It continues to be a major tourist attraction.

1863 Katherine Prescott Wormeley established a clothing factory in Newport, Rhode Island, which produced over 50,000 shirts for the Union Army.

1881 Clara Barton founded the American Red Cross.

1905 Winifred Holt and her sister Edith started the New York Association for the Blind. In 1923, Winifred founded the first "Lighthouse," which provided employment and recreation work for people who are blind.

1906 Madame C. J. Walker began selling hair-care products and cosmetics geared specifically to black women. She eventually became a millionaire.

1914 Elizabeth Arden founded her cosmetics company—now a multi-million-dollar empire.

1921 Juliette Low founded the Girl Scouts of America in Savannah, Georgia.

1924 Ida Rosenthal hired her husband to mass-produce brassieres, establishing Maidenform, Inc.

1933 Critic, author, and teacher Virginia Kirkus launched *Kirkus Reviews,* a publication that gave bookshop owners a preview and critique of books to aid them in deciding what to order. *Kirkus Reviews* is still used by thousands of bookstore owners and librarians nationwide today.

1938 Margaret Fogarty Rudkins launched her baking company, Pepperidge Farms, in Connecticut.

1944 Helen Valentine founded *Seventeen* magazine and served as editor in chief until 1950.

1945 Ruth Handler and her husband Elliot cofounded Mattel, Inc., with Harold Matson. Fifteen years later, she created the famous Barbie doll, named after her daughter. (It became Mattel's best-selling toy.)

1945 Helene Gordon founded and became the first editor in chief of *Elle* magazine in Paris.

1946 Eileen Ford founded the New York City modeling agency, Ford Models, Inc.

1946 Estée Lauder and her husband founded the New York cosmetics company bearing her name. They also pioneered the free sampling technique.

1950 Marjorie Child Husted, the creator of "Betty Crocker," left General Mills to form her own consulting company, Marjorie Husted and Associates, to advise other businesses on women's interests and activities.

1963 Jean Nidetch, who had battled compulsive overeating, founded Weight Watchers, Inc., to help other women develop healthy eating habits.

1963 Mary Kay Ash founded her Dallas-based company Mary Kay Cosmetics. The company has created opportunities for thousands of women to succeed in their own businesses selling her cosmetics.

1967 Muriel Siebert opened Muriel Siebert & Company, New York's first female-owned discount stock brokerage firm.

1968 Susie Tompkins started her fashion company, Esprit de Corps, making deliveries out of her station wagon in San Francisco.

1969 Judi Shepard Missett pioneered the first casual dance class for fitness, which launched her company, Jazzercise, Inc.

1969 Jessica McClintock founded Jessica McClintock Fashions, which now sells women's and children's clothing, bridal fashions, and perfumes through fourteen company-owned franchises as well as retailers.

1970 Barbara Gardner Proctor founded Proctor and Gardner Advertising after being fired from another agency for refusing to do an ad campaign she felt was morally wrong. Her company is now one of the most respected marketing companies in the country.

1972 Gloria Steinem and Patricia Carbine, noted feminist leaders, founded *Ms.* magazine in New York.

1973 Maryles V. Casto began Casto Travel, in Silicon Valley, California. Casto Travel is now one of largest travel agencies and event planners in the country.

1974 Joyce Meskis opened Tattered Cover Books, Inc., in Denver. It is now one of the largest bookstores in the country, boasting over 155,000 titles.

1975 Lois Geraci-Ernst began her New York firm, Advertising to Women, Inc., which focuses on the development and marketing of products for women.

1975 West German Anette Van Dorp founded an all-natural, environmentally safe lawn-trimming enterprise, Natural Lawn Trimming.

1976 Californian Joan Barnes launched her children's clothing business, Gymboree Corporation.

1976 Gail Koff opened her first storefront legal clinic, Jacoby & Myers, in New York City. There is now a chain of 110 Jacoby & Myers clinics across New York, New Jersey, Connecticut, Pennsylvania, Arizona, and California.

1976 Elizabeth Claiborne Ortenberg founded Liz Claiborne, Inc., which supplies sportswear merchandise to over 3,000 specialty stores and retailers.

1976 Anita Roddick founded the Body Shop in London. The Body Shop presently operates a chain of over 1,000 cosmetic retail stores worldwide.

1977 Debbi Fields founded the cookie company bearing her name. There are now over 700 Mrs. Fields Cookies stores throughout the United States, Europe, and the Far East.

1977 Kay Koplovitz founded MSG Sports Network in New York City. In 1980, MSG Sports Network became the USA Network.

1978 Phyllis Haeger began her Chicago association management company, Haeger & Associates. She is the founder of the Committee of 200, an honor society for women in business, and the founder of the National Association of Women Business Owners.

1978 Clara Taylor Reed founded Mid-Delta Home Health Inc., which provides health care services to the elderly and ill in the Mississippi Delta.

1980 Housewife-turned-entrepreneur Lin W. Lan launched Pacific Pioneer Insurance Company in Artesia, California.

1980 Cuba native Maria Elena Torano founded the Miami business bearing her name. Maria Elena Torano & Associates provides management consulting and environmental cleanup services to corporations and government agencies.

1981 Caroline Hirsch opened Caroline's Comedy Club and Pinky Ring Productions in New York City. She has since opened an additional comedy club in Los Angeles.

1982 Inspired by her own pregnancy, Rebecca Matthias founded her Philadelphia-based maternity clothing company, Mother's Work, Inc.

1983 Jenny Craig founded her weight loss company, Jenny Craig International, in Del Mar, California.

1983 Judy Sims left her position as a CPA to found Software Spectrum Corporation in Austin, Texas, which resells computer software to businesses nationwide.

1984 Fashion designer Donna Karan launched her own company, Donna Karan New York.

1984 June Morris founded Morris Airlines in Salt Lake City, which provides discount airfares to travelers in the Western United States.

1986 Oprah Winfrey formed HARPO Productions in Chicago to produce films, videos, and television movies.

1987 Theadora Barker of Carrollton, Texas, opened Beltline Mechanical Services, which installs and services air conditioning systems, after her employer denied her a promotion, saying that the servicemen wouldn't take orders from a woman and that contractors wouldn't work with a woman. (She ended up hiring six of those same servicemen.)

1987 Sheri Poe founded RYKA, Inc., in Norwood, Massachusetts. The company develops and produces women's athletic shoes.

1988 Linda D. Sonnatag founded SyStemix, Inc., in Palo Alto, California, which pioneers new therapies for treating blood diseases.

1989 Lisa A. Conte founded Shaman Pharmaceuticals, a California company that emphasizes drug discovery and creates an economic incentive to preserve rain forests.

1989 Tomina Edmark designed and marketed a hairstyling product called Topsytail, a patented plastic loop that helps make inverted-twist ponytails. Annual sales are estimated at forty million dollars.

1991 Colombia native Maria Elena Ibanez founded Internation Technology in Miami, which specializes in providing computer-related products and information to third-world countries.

1993 Gelly Borromeo started *Asian Entrepreneur* magazine.

1995 Carol Jackson Mouyiaris founded Bio Cosmetic Research Labs, which produces Black Opal cosmetics.

More Resources for Young Entrepreneurs

Y OU CAN FIND MANY PUBLICATIONS THAT OFFER ADVICE ON STARTING and running a company, succeeding in the world of business, making money, being a strong leader, and getting ahead. There are books, newsletters, and magazines that can provide the information you're looking for. You can also contact organizations and associations that specialize in business, entrepreneurship, money management, and leadership opportunities. Many of these organizations have their own publications and Web sites so you can learn more about their activities. Following is a list of resources that may help you to get ideas for launching your own business and making it a success.

Books

Alexander, S., *Women's Ventures, Women's Visions: Twenty-nine Inspiring Stories from Women Who Started Their Own Businesses* (Freedom, CA: The Crossing Press, 1997). The author has profiled twenty-nine remarkable women who found ways to establish their own businesses and realize their dreams. Read about their visions and personal triumphs.

Barkin, C., and E. James, *Jobs for Kids* (NY: Lothrop, Lee & Shepard Books, 1990). This book answers questions young people have about earning their own money and highlights jobs for youth—taking care of children and pets, doing yard work, running errands, tutoring, selling homemade products, and working for parents.

Berg, A. G., and A. B. Bochner, *The Totally Awesome Business Book for Kids—And Their Parents* (NY: Newmarket Press, 1997). A financial expert and her twelve-year-old son suggest twenty super businesses for kids ages ten to seventeen, with special attention to jobs that help the environment.
— *The Totally Awesome Business Book for Kids: With Twenty Super Businesses You Can Start Right Now!* (NY: Newmarket Press, 1995). Lots of colorful illustrations and easy-to-understand explanations provide a useful guide to earning money. Written by a financial expert and her twelve-year-old son, the book discusses business basics and the skills needed to run an office or a business. Fun activities are also included.

Bernstein, D., *Better Than a Lemonade Stand! Small Business Ideas for Kids* (Hillsboro, OR: Beyond Words Publishing, Inc., 1992). This illustrated book contains fifty-one ideas young people can use to start their own small business. Fifteen-year-old author Daryl Bernstein provides a good list of concerns and possible pitfalls, as well as words of encouragement for young entrepreneurs.
— *The Venture Adventure: Your Career As an Entrepreneur* (Hillsboro, OR: Beyond Words Publishing, Inc., 1996). This guide is from the young author who created *Better Than a Lemonade Stand* (above). It shows readers how to turn their vision into venture capital, and includes strategies and secrets for creating a booming business.

Bodnar, J., *Money-Smart Kids (and Parents, Too!)* (Washington, D.C.: Kiplinger Books, 1993). This book contains chapters on allowances, saving, investing, collecting, earning money, and managing finances. Written mainly for parents, the book also includes sections about protecting children's financial interests with life insurance and wills. Share the book with a parent or another adult.

Cook, J., *Usborne Introduction to Business* (London: Usborne Publishing, Ltd., 1985). This colorfully illustrated guide contains brief explanations of business topics such as selling, bookkeeping, legal issues, borrowing money, taxation, stocks, exporting, marketing, and building a business empire. Success stories are also included.

Drew, B., and N. Drew, *Fast Cash for Kids* (Franklin Lake, NJ: Career Press, 1995). In this book, you'll learn the how to's of business: how to think like an entrepreneur, how to find an idea, how to turn an idea into a business, how to attract customers, how to handle money, and how to be your own boss. Start-up ideas for small businesses and educational resources are also listed.

Godfrey, J., *No More Frogs to Kiss* (NY: Harper Business, 1995). Designed to empower girls economically, this book lists ninety-nine ways girls can earn money and exercise their financial power. Includes local and national business opportunities for girls and women.

Greene, I., *How to Be a Success in Business* (San Diego: People Skills International, 1995). This book presents ways to become a successful businessperson and to be more effective in the workplace.

Iannarelli, C., and J. Iannarelli, *The ABC's of Business: With Emily and the Entrekids* (Greensburg, PA: Seton Hill College, 1994). This fictional tale leads readers on a journey with Emily, as she travels to different businesses started by children. The book introduces basic business concepts, including advertising, money, risk, and capital.

Iannarelli, C., and W. Peters, *The Adventure of Entrepreneurship: A Journey to Self-Discovery for Young Women* (Greensburg, PA: Seton Hill College, 1987). This workbook for young women explores entrepreneurship, personal planning, professional image, gender roles, goal setting, communication, and career opportunities.

Jones, V. L., *Kids Can Make Money Too! How Young People Can Succeed Financially: Over 200 Ways to Earn Money and How to Make It Grow* (Los Angeles: Calico Paws, 1988). This guide for children (and their parents) covers the basics: checking accounts, credit card traps, business start-up ideas, etc. Some interesting financial ideas are explored, such as getting paid twice and making money while you sleep.

Karnes, F. A., and S. M. Bean, *Girls and Young Women Inventing: Twenty True Stories About Inventors Plus How You Can Be One Yourself* (Minneapolis: Free Spirit Publishing, Inc., 1995). Inventing is a great way to create a unique product for a business. In this collection of true stories, readers learn about getting ideas, thinking creatively, and applying for a patent. Includes step-by-step information about the inventing process.
— *Girls and Young Women Leading the Way: Twenty True Stories About Leadership* (Minneapolis: Free Spirit Publishing, Inc., 1993). These narratives of girls and young women who have taken on positions of leadership prove that anyone can be a leader, business or otherwise. A leadership handbook section is also included.

Lamancusa, J., *Kid Cash: Creative Money-Making Ideas* (Blue Ridge Summit, PA: TAB Books, 1993). This book includes forty chapters on money-making ideas for youth and discusses job descriptions, start-up costs, price setting, and reaching a target audience. The author even provides examples of brochures and flyers that readers can duplicate for their own advertising.

Leedy, L., *The Monster Money Book* (NY: Holiday House, Inc., 1996). Disguised as a tale about the antics of the "money monsters," this book offers young readers practical information on being smart shoppers. Readers explore the concepts of making a budget, borrowing, investing, and using a checking and savings account.

McWhorter, A., *An Introduction to Business for African-American Youth* (Detroit: Xpression Publishing, 1995). Author and entrepreneur Abner McWhorter, who opened a framing business at the age of seventeen, created this book to help other African American youth to become self-sufficient and successful in the business world. The author provides advice, tips, and powerful examples of other successful African Americans.

Menzies, L., *Teens' Guide to Business: The Secret to a Successful Enterprise* (NY: MasterMedia Limited, 1995). Filled with tips and interactive quizzes, this book also features business role models from different areas of the country and from various ethnic and economic backgrounds. Ways to succeed in business are presented in an easy-to-understand, fun format.

Otfinoski, S., *The Kid's Guide to Money: Earning It, Saving It, Spending It, Growing It, Sharing It* (NY: Scholastic, Inc., 1996). This illustrated guide covers money matters (earning, spending, banking, sharing, borrowing, etc.) that young people should consider before they earn their first dollar. Includes a list of organizations that may be helpful for young people learning to manage their money.

Riehm, S., *The Teenage Entrepreneur's Guide: 50 Money-Making Business Ideas* (Chicago: Surrey Books, 1990). This guide offers fifty time-tested businesses that teens can start and run on their own, with a minimum investment of time and money. Most of these businesses can be run from home or in the neighborhood.

Sheffer, S., Ed., *Earning Our Own Money: Homeschoolers 13 and Under Describe How They Have Earned Money* (Cambridge, MA: Holt & Associates, 1991). This book contains inspiring stories about ways young people have earned money. Common money-making methods, as well as unusual jobs and ideas, are included.

Slovacek, C., *Open for Business: A Simulation for Student-Run Enterprises* (San Luis Obispo, CA: Dandy Lion Publications, 1996). This resource guide is designed to help teachers implement an introductory course in owning and running a business. Share this resource with your teacher to help start a course in your school. Includes activities, handouts, and an informal assessment.

Thompson, T., *Biz Kids' Guide to Success: Money-Making Ideas for Young Entrepreneurs* (Hauppauge, NY: Barron's Educational Series, Inc., 1992). Young entrepreneurs can use this illustrated guide to follow the steps needed to start a business and to market their product or service. Includes a useful glossary of business terms.

Magazines and Newsletters

Kids' Wall Street News. Call (760) 591-7681 for information on subscribing. This news and financial publication for youth has articles on young entrepreneurs, business know-how, money and banking, computers and technology, and much more.

Turned On Business, published by An Income of Her Own. Call 1-800-350-2978 for information on subscribing. This publication has articles on female entrepreneurs, plus news bits and reviews of magazines and Web sites for girls.

Young Entrepreneur, published by KidsWay, Inc. Call 1-888-KidsWay (1-888-543-7929) for information on subscribing. Each issue features business how-to advice from young people who operate their own businesses. Your first issue is free.

Zillions, published by Consumers Union (which also publishes *Consumer Reports*). Write to: Zillions, P.O. Box 54861, Boulder, CO 80322-4861 for subscription service. This winner of the EdPress award for excellence in educational journalism helps readers to become educated consumers. Learn about products that work and don't work, money management, and advertising gimmicks aimed at kids.

Organizations and Associations

An Income of Her Own (AIOHO)
1804 W. Burbank Boulevard
Burbank, CA 91506
1-800-350-2978
http://www.anincomeofherown.com
Devoted to supporting the economic empowerment of young women, AIOHO provides the tools, knowledge, and experience to help girls gain financial independence. AIOHO sponsors business plan competitions and a business camp for teens (Camp $tart-Up), publishes a newsletter called *Turned On Business,* and provides a support network and resources for female entrepreneurs.

Association of Black Women Entrepreneurs (ABWE)
P.O. Box 49368
Los Angeles, CA 90049
(213) 624-8639
This nonprofit association strives to increase networking, education, business contacts, and opportunities for African American women. ABWE also supports the education of children.

Association of Small Business Development Centers (ASBDC)
1300 Chain Bridge Road, Suite 201
McLean, VA 22101
(703) 448-6124
FAX: (703) 448-6125
More than fifty ASBDC centers across the nation offer seminars and other training to help small businesses to succeed. Supporting special groups, including young entrepreneurs, is an important part of their mission.

Business and Professional Women/USA
2012 Massachusetts Avenue NW
Washington, D.C. 20036
(202) 293-1100
FAX: (202) 861-0298
Sponsors of the Young Careerist Program, this association offers the opportunity to meet and network with young entrepreneurs in the early stages of their careers.

Business Cents Resources
3038 Washington Pike
Bridgeville, PA 15017
1-800-67-CINDY (1-800-672-4639)
FAX: (412) 221-0150
Business Cents Resources offers a host of educational resources to assist children and adults in learning more about business and entrepreneurship. The organization also sponsors Camp Business Cents, a youth summer camp.

Business Professionals of America (BPA)
5454 Cleveland Avenue
Columbus, OH 43231
(614) 895-7277
FAX: (614) 895-1165
http://www.bpa.org/bpa.html
The mission of this organization is to prepare a world-class workforce by strengthening leadership, citizenship, academic, and technical skills in learners of all ages. BPA hosts competitive events for students in business education, as well as an awards program.

Children's Financial Network, Inc.
70 Tower Hill Road
Mountain Lakes, NJ 07046
(201) 335-6929
FAX: (201) 334-5380
This network publishes books and articles to help adults and children to gain a better understanding of finances, money, and business.

Communities in Schools
1199 North Fairfax Street, Suite 300
Alexandria, VA 22314
(703) 519-8999
FAX: (703) 519-7213
http://www.cisnet.org
There are several Communities in Schools affiliates across America, all of which aim to reduce the high school dropout rate by piloting programs that teach kids about entrepreneurship.

Distributive Education Clubs of America (DECA)
1908 Association Drive
Reston, VA 20191
(703) 860-5000
FAX: (703) 860-4013
http://www.deca.org
DECA is a national association of marketing students, with chapters in many high schools across the United States. Through this program, young people can network and share strategies for effective business practices.

Do Something
423 West 55th Street, 8th Floor
New York, NY 10019
(212) 978-7777
FAX: (212) 582-1309
http://www.dosomething.org
This national nonprofit organization encourages young people to apply entrepreneurial skills to solve problems in their community. Other notable

activities include local grant programs, sponsorship of community coaches, and leadership courses.

Educational, Training and Enterprise Center (EDTEC)
313 Market Street
Camden, NJ 08102
(609) 342-8277
FAX: (609) 963-8110
http://www.edtecinc.com
Through classroom instruction, EDTEC encourages kids to become entrepreneurs. The organization also offers staff training and technical assistance to schools and other organizations interested in teaching youth entrepreneurship.

The Entrepreneurial Development Institute (TEDI)
20251 I Street NW, Suite 905
Washington, D.C. 20006
(202) 822-8334
http://www.bedrock.com/tedi/hometxt.html
TEDI empowers disadvantaged youth by teaching them how to think like entrepreneurs. The program promotes small business development, academic skills, and positive attitudes.

First Nations Development Institute
The Stores Building
11917 Main Street
Fredericksburg, VA 22408
(540) 371-5615
FAX: (540) 371-3505
With a main objective of encouraging economic development on Indian reservations, the Institute provides seed money and technical assistance to young American Indians who want to start and run their own businesses.

Future Business Leaders of America (FBLA)
1912 Association Drive
Reston, VA 20191
(703) 860-3334
FAX: (703) 758-0749
http://www.fbla-pbl.org
An educational organization for middle and high school students, the FBLA strives to prepare students for careers in business and business-related fields. This organization is called Phi Beta Lambda in colleges.

Institute for Youth Entrepreneurship
310 Lenox Avenue, 2nd Floor
New York, NY 10027
(212) 369-3900
FAX: (212) 369-5369

This community-owned initiative provides comprehensive instruction and work-related experiences for program participants, ages twelve to eighteen. This model combines mentorship with two components: the classroom and the living business.

Junior Achievement
One Education Way
Colorado Springs, CO 80906
(719) 540-8000
FAX: (719) 540-6299
http://www.ja.org
More than two million strong, students in Junior Achievement plan and set up business simulations with the help of business executives from across the country. Through the program, students of all ages learn the basics of the private enterprise system.

Kids Venture
7201 Haven Avenue, Suite E-325
Alta Loma, CA 91701
(909) 948-5891
FAX: (909) 948-5991
Kids Venture sells videos and books about entrepreneurship for children.

KidsWay, Inc.
5585 Peachtree Road
Chamblee, GA 30341
1-888-KidsWay (1-888-543-7929)
The goal of this organization is to give young people hands-on experience in the world of business through education and entrepreneurship training. KidsWay publishes a newsletter called *Young Entrepreneur* and offers summer job kits for young people interested in babysitting, car washing, pet care, and odd jobs. The kits include instructions for finding customers, managing records, and working safely.

Minority Youth Entrepreneurship Program
Washington University
John M. Olin School of Business
Campus Box 1133
1 Brookings Drive
St. Louis, MO 63130-4899
(314) 935-4218
FAX: (314) 935-4464
Designed to expose high school minority youth to the advantages of self-employment, this program teaches students basic business skills in accounting, finance, economics, writing, and research. Local minority business owners give speeches and presentations to inspire youth involved in the program to consider entrepreneurship.

National Center for American Indian Enterprise Development
953 East Juanita Avenue
Mesa, AZ 85204
(602) 545-1298
FAX: (602) 545-4208
This center serves as a management consulting firm to American Indians and focuses on entrepreneurial education. Through their programs, young American Indians can meet with American Indian businesspeople to learn about business basics and the benefits of entrepreneurship.

National Education Center for Women in Business (NECWB)
Seton Hill Drive
Greensburg, PA 15601-1599
1-800-NECWB-4-U (1-800-632-9248)
FAX: (412) 834-7131
http://www.necwb.setonhill.edu
The mission of this center is to promote women and business leadership on the national level. The Center sponsors two youth camps: Camp Entrepreneur Adventure, a five-day program for teen girls that encourages business ownership, and Camp Entrepreneur Executive, which provides the teen daughters of business owners with the training needed to take over the family business.

National Foundation for Teaching Entrepreneurship (NFTE)
120 Wall Street, 29th Floor
New York, NY 10005
(212) 232-3333
FAX: (212) 232-2244
NFTE offers entrepreneurial training to students from low-income communities.

National 4-H Council
7100 Connecticut Avenue
Chevy Chase, MD 20815
(301) 961-2818
FAX: (301) 961-2894
http://www.fourhcouncil.edu
The National 4-H Council offers local and national programs designed to encourage young people to consider entrepreneurship as a career. It also sponsors Revitalizing Rural America, a program to help young people start businesses in rural areas.

One to One Partnership, Inc.
2801 M Street NW
Washington, D.C. 20007
(202) 338-3844
FAX: (202) 338-1642
Created by leading philanthropists, businesspeople, educators, and entrepreneurs, this partnership is dedicated to bringing the power of mentoring to more children. It spon-

sors the Institute for Youth Entrepreneurship and has affiliates in eleven major metropolitan communities.

Operation Enterprise
American Management Association
P.O. Box 88
West Lake Marine Road
Hamilton, NY 13346
1-800-634-4262
(315) 824-2000
FAX: (315) 824-6710
American Management Association sponsors Operation Enterprise, a program offering a ten-day entrepreneurship workshop to high school students ages sixteen and up. The program focuses on entrepreneurship, personal growth, professional success, and self-motivation.

Rural Entrepreneurship through Action Learning
(REAL Enterprises)
115 Market Street, Suite 320
Durham, NC 27701-3221
1-800-798-0643
FAX: (919) 682-7621
Sixteen states currently participate in REAL Enterprises, a program that establishes entrepreneurship courses in rural high schools. The program also encourages partnerships between school systems, local businesses, and community groups.

Service Corps of Retired Executives (SCORE)
c/o Small Business Administration (SBA)
406 Third Street SW
Washington, D.C. 20416
1-800-8-ASK-SBA (1-800-827-5722)
FAX: (202) 205-7064
http://www.sba.gov
Sponsored by the SBA, this organization consists of more than 13,000 retired and semi-retired business executives. Its mission is to offer small businesses free advice. (Aspiring entrepreneurs of all ages can call for helpful hints.)

Small Business Administration
406 Third Street SW
Washington, D.C. 20416
1-800-8-ASK-SBA (1-800-827-5722)
FAX: (202) 205-7064
http://www.sba.gov
With a branch office in every state, the SBA can assist entrepreneurs of any age with every aspect of starting a business—from planning, to finding capital, to marketing a product, and to managing employees.

Trickle-Up Program
54 Riverside Drive
New York, NY 10024
(212) 362-7958
FAX: (212) 877-7464
http://www.vita.org/trickle/trickle.html
The Trickle-Up Program pairs volunteers with high school students in inner-city neighborhoods who want to start businesses. It also offers business training programs, and even small start-up capital, to students.

Volunteers of America
Midas Touch Program
3600 Wilshire Boulevard, Suite 1500
Los Angeles, CA 90010
(213) 389-1500
FAX: (213) 385-7599
Designed to teach young people the fundamentals of the free enterprise system and the social responsibilities of business, this program pairs youth with mentors who can guide and advise them as they start their new businesses.

Young Americans Education Foundation
311 Steele Street
Denver, CO 80206
(303) 321-2954
FAX: (303) 320-6507
The mission of this nonprofit foundation is to teach children how to handle finances responsibly. One program offered by the Foundation is Be Your Own Boss, which highlights entrepreneurship.

Young Entrepreneurs Network
376 Boylston Street, Suite 304
Boston, MA 02116
(617) 867-4690
FAX: (617) 267-3057
http://www.idye.com
This association is an international network of aspiring, emerging, and successful business owners from over forty countries. Created to help younger entrepreneurs to build their own business networks at an early age, the Network has active publishing and consulting divisions, a line of business resources and services, and a site on the World Wide Web.

Glossary

Bookkeeping: The practice of recording the accounts and transactions of a business. Your records may include *cash receipts* (money taken in), *cash disbursements* (money paid out), *accounts receivable* (a record of money owed to your company), *accounts payable* (what your business owes to any creditors or suppliers), plus sales (daily and monthly), payroll, equipment, and inventory.

Capital: Wealth in the form of money or property, used or accumulated in a business by a person, a partnership, or a corporation.

Cash flow: The flow of money, in terms of income and payments, from a person or a company.

Client: The party for whom services are rendered; a customer.

Collateral: Property that has been pledged by a borrower to protect the interests of the lender. Types of business and personal collateral can include savings accounts, inventory, equipment, or stocks and bonds.

Consignment: *(on consignment)* The provision that payment is expected only on completed sales and that any unsold items may be returned to the person who is consigning. If you want to sell your product on consignment, the usual procedure is that you determine the price and the store will take a consignment percentage—you get the remaining percentage if your product sells. (Make sure you get the agreement in writing.)

Contract: An agreement between two or more parties, especially one that is written and enforceable by law.

Copyright: The legal right granted to the originator of a creative work (author, artist, composer, playwright, or publisher, for example) to exclusively produce, sell, or distribute the work.

Corporation: A group of individuals formed and authorized by law to act as a single entity, with its own rights, privileges, and duties. A corporation must follow state laws, and it must be set up according to the legal procedures of the state within which it is formed.

Cost of goods sold (COGS): The costs of producing your specific products or services.

Debt: Something owed, such as money, goods, or services.

Focus group: A small group selected from a wider population. The purpose of the group is to sample (through open discussion) the members' opinions about or responses to a particular product or subject.

For-profit business: A business that is established or operated with the intention of making a profit.

General partnership: Two or more people become owners of a business, and they each have the right to manage the business and share in the profits. When forming a partnership, the parties should protect themselves by writing up an agreement stating each partner's duties, rights, obligations, financial contributions, etc.

Gross profit: The total sales revenue less (minus) the cost to produce goods or services.

Income: The amount of money received during a period of time in exchange for a person's labor or services, from the sale of goods or property, or as profit from financial investments.

Incorporate: To form into a legal corporation. When incorporating, the people involved must file "articles of incorporation" with their state.

Interest: A charge for a loan, usually a percentage of the amount loaned.

Inventory: The quantity of goods and materials on hand; a detailed and itemized list of things in one's possession.

Investor: One who commits money or capital in order to gain a financial return.

Limited partnership: A business partnership in which one or more of the partners has limited liability to the extent of the amount of money they have invested in the business. To form a limited partnership, the parties should consult a lawyer for technical help and must file with the state.

Logo: A name, symbol, or trademark designed for easy and definite recognition.

Mail order: An order for goods to be shipped through the mail.

Market: A part of the population considered as buyers for a product or service; the opportunity to buy and sell; the extent of the demand for merchandise or services.

Marketing: the functions (advertising, publicity, distributors, promotions, etc.) involved in transferring goods from producer to consumer.

Mentor: A trusted advisor or teacher.

Net profit: The gross profit less (minus) payments for wages, rent, bills, interest to be paid on loans, etc. (Your taxes are paid on net profit.)

Networking: Forming and keeping in touch with an extended group of people who have similar interests and concerns, to assist and support one another.

Nonprofit business: A business or organization that is *not* established or operated with the intention of making a profit.

Overhead: Of or relating to the operating expenses of a business (rent, interest payments on loans, etc.).

Patent: An authorization made by the government that gives a creator of an invention the right to make, use, and sell that invention for a certain period of time.

Press release: An announcement of an event or other newsworthy item, issued to the press. A business owner may send out a press release about new products or a grand opening, for example.

Profit: *See* Gross profit, Net profit.

Revenue: The total income produced by a business.

Sole proprietorship: A business owned by one person. The sole proprietor is usually responsible for all of the day-to-day operations and business decisions.

Tax-exempt: Not subject to being taxed.

Trademark: A name, symbol, or other device that identifies a product. A trademark is officially registered and, by law, restricted to use by the owner.

Wholesale: The sale of goods in large quantities for resale by a retailer.

Word-of-mouth: Spoken communication. People may hear of your business by word-of-mouth, meaning from your clients or satisfied customers.

Index

A

The ABC's of Business (Iannarelli and Iannarelli), 167

ABWE. *See* Association of Black Women Entrepreneurs (ABWE)

Addition and Subtraction Hair Firm, 96–99

Address book, 5

The Adventure of Entrepreneurship (Iannarelli and Peters), 167

Advertising. *See* Marketing

African Americans, 1–2, 151

Age, of entrepreneur, 123

AIOHO. *See* An Income of Her Own (AIOHO)

Alexander, S., 165

An Income of Her Own (AIOHO), 170

    National Teen Business Plan Competition, 108–111, 121

Animals. *See* Pet-Sitting Club (PSC)

Arbor Day, 115

Art. *See* specific art form, e.g. Painting

Arthritis, and Wristies, 33

Arts and crafts. *See* Crafts

ASBDC. *See* Association of Small Business Development Centers (ASBDC)

Ash, Mary Kay, 153

Association of Black Women Entrepreneurs (ABWE), 170

Association of Small Business Development Centers (ASBDC), 170

Aten, J., 157

Awareness, 155

B

Baar, Mandy, 83–88, *84, 86, 87*

Babysitters Club, 78

Baily, Beth, 78–82, *79, 80, 81*

Baily, Theresa ,78–82, *79, 80, 81*

Bakeries, 83–88

Barclay, Jennifer Paige, 154

Barkin, C., 165

Bean, S. M., 167, 191

Beauty care. *See* Cosmetics; Hair care

Bell, Danyel, 25–28, *26*

Ben and Jerry (Greenburg), 157

Ben and Jerry's ice cream, 156

Benefits of entrepreneurship, 129

Berg, A. G., 166

Bergson, Shilcock, 60–67, *61, 62, 65*

Bernstein, D., 166

Better Than a Lemonade Stand! (Bernstein), 166

Biz Kids' Guide to Success (Thompson), 169

Blue Fish Clothing, 154

Blue Jeans (Weidt), 159

Bochner, A. B., 166

Bodnar, J., 166

Bookkeeping, defined, 177

About the Authors

*F*RANCES KARNES RECEIVED HER PH.D. IN EDUCATION FROM THE UNIVERSITY of Illinois. She is currently Professor of Special Education at the University of Southern Mississippi and has been part of the university faculty for over two decades. She is Director of the Center for Gifted Studies and the center's Director of the Leadership Studies Program for grades 6–11.

Frances is past president of The Association for the Gifted, a national organization, and the founder and first president of the Mississippi Association for the Gifted. She has coauthored twelve books and more than 160 journal articles on a variety of subjects, including girls, leadership, gifted children, and legal issues. Frances resides in Hattiesburg, Mississippi, with her husband, Dr. M. Ray Karnes. Family members are Christopher, John, Leighanne, and Mary Ryan Karnes.

*S*UZANNE BEAN RECEIVED HER B.S. IN ELEMENTARY EDUCATION FROM DELTA State University in Mississippi and earned her M.Ed. and Ph.D. in Special Education (with an emphasis in Gifted Education) from the University of Southern Mississippi. She is currently an associate professor of education at the Mississippi University for Women in Columbus. She has served as Director of the Mississippi Governor's School, a residential program for high school students who show high intellectual, creative, and leadership potential. She has also served as Vice Chair of the National Conference on Governor's Schools.

Suzanne has served as President of the Mississippi Association of Talented and Gifted and has participated in numerous conference and workshop presentations. She is also a consultant in the area of education of the gifted. Suzanne and her husband, Dr. Mark H. Bean, have a daughter, Cameron Meriweather, and a son, Mark Hudson.

Frances and Suzanne have also written *Girls and Young Women Leading the Way: Twenty True Stories About Leadership* and *Girls and Young Women Inventing: Twenty True Stories About Inventors Plus How You Can Be One Yourself* for Free Spirit Publishing.

Other Great Books from Free Spirit Publishing

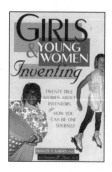

GIRLS AND YOUNG WOMEN INVENTING
Twenty True Stories About Inventors *Plus* How You Can Be One Yourself
by Frances A. Karnes, Ph.D., and Suzanne M. Bean, Ph.D.
Not just for girls and young women, this book will inspire *all* young people to think more creatively. Part 1 features first-person stories of successful young inventors. Part 2 includes step-by-step instructions on how to be an inventor, from creative problem solving to developing a marketing plan. Part 3 presents information about inventors' associations and organizations, a timeline of women inventors, quotations, and recommended readings.
$12.95; 176 pp.; s/c; B&W photos; 6" x 9"
ISBN 0-915793-89-X; ages 11 & up

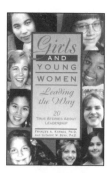

GIRLS AND YOUNG WOMEN LEADING THE WAY
Twenty True Stories About Leadership
by Frances A. Karnes, Ph.D., and Suzanne M. Bean, Ph.D.
First-person stories by girls and young women prove that anyone can be a leader, regardless of gender or age. Written in the same format as *Girls and Young Women Inventing*, this book also includes a how-to "Leadership Handbook" section.
$11.95; 168 pp.; s/c; B&W photos; 6" x 9"
ISBN 0-915793-52-0; ages 11 & up

TOTALLY PRIVATE AND PERSONAL
Journaling Ideas for Girls and Young Women
by Young Author Jessica Wilber
Reading this book is like sharing the experience of journaling with a smart, witty, understanding (and totally cool) best friend. Teen author Jessica Wilber is a dedicated journaler. Her personal insights, experiences, and guidance—including hundreds of journaling tips and suggestions, advice about growing up and being a girl, ideas for fun things to do, resources (books, magazines, Web sites), glimpses into her own journals, and more—speak directly to readers, making journaling more meaningful and fun.
$8.95; 168 pp.; s/c; 5⅛" x 7⅞"
ISBN 1-57542-005-8; ages 11–16

Find these books in your favorite bookstore, or write or call:

Free Spirit Publishing Inc.
400 First Avenue North, Suite 616
Minneapolis, MN 55401-1724
Toll-free (800) 735-7323, Local (612) 338-2068
help4kids@freespirit.com